Praise for *Adopting the Rational Unified Process*

"Stefan Bergström and Lotta Råberg take you through what may be your most crucial step in using the Rational Unified Process: a successful adoption process. From assessment of your current capability to the details of RUP implementation, this book takes you by the hand, and guides you. It is all backed by their considerable practical experience helping major industrial companies in Europe implement RUP."

—*PHILIPPE KRUCHTEN,*
IBM Rational Software

"This book provides a unique perspective on how to successfully introduce lasting improvements into any software development organization. It provides practical guidance into how to conduct a process improvement effort using the Rational Unified Process, written by people who have many years of experience helping customers to be successful with RUP. This book is an essential addition to the bookshelf of anyone adopting RUP, or undertaking any software engineering process improvement effort."

—*KURT BITTNER,*
Worldwide Communities of Practice
Architect, IBM Rational Software
Co-author of Use Case Modeling,
Addison-Wesley, 2003

"*Adopting the Rational Unified Process* offers real-world advice from those who have been there, implementing RUP in enterprises and organizations. The authors speak from a deep, practical knowledge and honestly share both their successes and mistakes. Following the guidance in this book could save you months or years of costly trial-and-error when implementing RUP."

—*BARCLAY BROWN,*
Renaissance Research Corp.

"Change is inevitable in the sometimes bleeding edge of software development; so where we can borrow best practices from other proven disciplines such as Business Change Management, we should do so with both hands. The authors practically demonstrate how to leverage these sensible practices when implementing the Rational Unified Process. If you are responsible for implementing RUP in your organization and can only buy one book, make it this one."

—*TONY GROUT,*
CEO, FMI Solutions

Adopting the Rational
Unified Process

The Addison-Wesley Object Technology Series

Grady Booch, Ivar Jacobson, and James Rumbaugh, Series Editors
For more information, check out the series web site at www.awprofessional.com/otseries.

The Component Software Series

Clemens Szyperski, Series Editor
For more information, check out the series web site at
www.awprofessional.com/csseries.

Adopting the Rational Unified Process

Success with the RUP

Stefan Bergström

Lotta Råberg

✦ Addison-Wesley

Boston · San Francisco · New York · Toronto · Montreal
London · Munich · Paris · Madrid
Capetown · Sydney · Tokyo · Singapore · Mexico City

The publisher offers discounts on this book when ordered in quantity for bulk purchases and special sales. For more information, please contact:

U.S. Corporate and Government Sales
(800) 382-3419
corpsales@pearsontechgroup.com

For sales outside of the U.S., please contact:

International Sales
(317) 581-3793
international@pearsontechgroup.com

Visit Addison-Wesley on the Web: www.awprofessional.com

Library of Congress Cataloging-in-Publication Data
Bergström, Stefan
    Adopting the Rational Unified Process : success with the RUP / Stefan Bergström, Lotta Råberg.
       p.   cm.
    Includes bibliographical references and index.
    ISBN 0-321-20294-5 (alk. paper)
    1. Computer software--Development. 2. Software engineering.   I. Råberg, Lotta.
 II. Title.

QA76.76.D47B4578 2003
005.1—dc22   2003062932

ISBN 0-321-20294-5
Text printed on recycled paper
1 2 3 4 5 6 7 8 9 10—CRS—0706050403
First printing, December 2003

Contents

Preface

Why Did We Write This Book?

Some things in life just seem to happen. Of course, writing a book needs to be planned in detail by the authors, but the starting point of the endeavor to write down our collective experience of helping customers implement the IBM Rational Unified Process (RUP) did not follow any schedule. Suddenly, after years of mentoring, preparing presentations, and writing papers and articles, it just felt like it was time to collect all that information in one place—to make a baseline.

There are many books about RUP, and some of them bring up implementation matters. Also, there are many books about process improvements in general as well as change in general. However, this is the first book that focuses solely on RUP implementation, that is, how to put RUP into practice.

Put RUP to Use!

RUP gives the software development community a common language and a base for a common, more controlled way to develop software. By writing this book we want to help the reader have a better experience working with RUP by suggesting methods of how to adopt it in the best way.

RUP will not yield its intended benefits if not successfully implemented. Succeeding with a RUP implementation can be hard. Although RUP has been around for a while now, some people still struggle with the best way to put RUP into practice. This is a pity because RUP contains so many excellent things! A good working environment for software developers is more than a good chair, a fast computer, and an ergonomic keyboard. A good working environment also encompasses a decent process and appropriate tools. There is no reason that software developers always should work more or less ad hoc. RUP has the answer. Unfortunately, it can be difficult for software developers in general to realize the value of RUP if it is not adopted properly. The power of RUP lies in its implementation!

It Is All about People

As for all initiatives for making business processes in which people work more effective, implementing RUP in an organization is all about people. Still, it is easy to underestimate the effort required to change the ways people think about their work. Even if an organization decides that RUP shall be used for all software development, it is hard to enforce that decision. By sharing our best practices with you in this book, we hope that organizations that implement RUP in the future will give the "people issues" the attention they deserve, and then plan the implementation accordingly. It is our firm belief that organizations will benefit even more from RUP as a result.

We have a strong belief in mentorship—in being fair and helping people to change. They need someone to show them how to do things the new way. People need someone to talk to. Before trying to adopt RUP on your own, use a RUP mentor to give you some hints and advice. This way, some common traps can be avoided, and you can use RUP efficiently from the start. A RUP implementation should not be based solely on a trial-and-error approach.

Who Will Benefit from This Book?

Who is responsible for the processes in an organization? Management? The project managers? The people working in the processes? We say that everyone is responsible. Of course, the formal responsibility will vary, but everyone just mentioned has a role in the processes and should feel responsible for their results. This book is intended for the following audiences:

- Managers who will be in charge of implementing RUP in an organization and/or one or more software development projects.
- Project managers who will both become RUP practitioners and are expected to support and sometimes drive the RUP implementation for the project members. People in this tough position will get support from this book.
- Project members who are RUP practitioners, that is, those who will start work according to RUP (following the guidance of any RUP discipline). This book will give new RUP practitioners a positive attitude toward RUP, which will ease their adoption of it.
- Process and method engineers who will be involved when customizing RUP, selecting subsets of it, and integrating it with other processes and methods.
- RUP mentors, that is, people who will help practitioners get started with RUP by transferring knowledge during actual work.
- Quality assurance professionals who are deeply concerned with processes and their definitions as well as with making sure that work adheres to set standards and is improved if needed.

What Is Not in This Book?

This is not an introductory book to RUP. It does not even talk much about the content in RUP, with the exception of the real-life examples. We want to focus on the process of implementing RUP. If you need information about what is in RUP, we recommend the Rational Unified Process product itself: *The Rational Unified Process, An Introduction, Third Edition* by Philippe Kruchten [2003], or *The Rational Unified Process Made Easy: A Practitioner's Guide to the RUP* by Per Kroll and Philippe Kruchten [2003].

Nor is this a book about organizational change in general. Such a book would probably include psychological theories and plenty of studies about human behavior during certain circumstances. We are self-taught and have no such academic background. We base our advice regarding how to proceed with the change of implementing a new process on our experiences only.

What about the Process Engineering Process?

This book could have been an introductory book to the Process Engineering Process (PEP) included in the RUP product, but it is not. Still, this book and PEP cover the same topic: how to adopt RUP in an organization for its software development projects. So what's the difference between the two? A process, like RUP or PEP, extensively sorts out *all* the roles, activities, and artifacts that should be involved when engineering software (RUP) or engineering a process (PEP). A book, like this one, may present and talk you through a sometimes overwhelming topic in pedagogical order to help create a deeper understanding, following the main thread.

There are no contradictions in terms of "things that need to be done" when adopting RUP as described in this book and when using PEP. But note that PEP includes a lot of support for *developing your own tailored process*, apart from "just" implementing things from standard RUP, as this book emphasizes. Still, Chapter 9, "Deciding upon Your Process," discusses the issues of selecting from RUP and adding process information to RUP, and Chapter 10, "Documenting Your Process," presents the options available (including tools) when documenting these decisions. This book is not at all as detailed as PEP. Therefore, read more about PEP—if not before, then at least after you have read this book. And do remember the "soft" aspects of implementing a process.

How This Book Is Organized

This book has eleven chapters plus two appendixes, a glossary and a recommended reading section. The obvious choice for approaching this book is to read it chapter by chapter in order. This will tell you how to adopt RUP in an organization. However, the book does not *have* to be read chapter by chapter. For example, you can start with Chapter 8, which will tell you how to adopt RUP in a single software development project. Cross-references will help you find other information related to what you read in particular chapters. We tried to write this book with a minimum of technical language, and we take a practical approach to the subject, basing all reasoning on our own experiences. Brief overviews of the chapters follow.

Chapter 1, How to Adopt RUP in Your Organization, throws you directly into the core topic of the book. This chapter presents a flow of activities that will make the adoption of RUP easier. This flow will also serve as a navigation tool for the rest of the book, where all activities will be revisited.

Chapter 2, The First Meeting with RUP, gives you a warm-up to the rest of the book through our simple explanation of what RUP is. If you are a practitioner, read this chapter in order to get a good understanding of RUP and an appropriate mind-set. If you are a RUP mentor, read this chapter to see how you can explain RUP to others.

Chapter 3, What Is a RUP Project?, delves into perhaps the most common question when it comes to usage of RUP. We give it an answer.

Chapter 4, Assessing Your Organization, explores how to find out how the organization develops software today as well as what is important to the organization when doing so.

Chapter 5, Motivating the RUP Adoption, discusses the need to motivate the adoption of RUP from an economical aspect as well as the need to motivate the receivers of the new process, that is, the employees in your organization.

Chapter 6, Planning the RUP Adoption, describes the concepts of setting goals, identifying risks and opportunities, and understanding the importance of communication—and, of course, how to plan for the RUP adoption.

Chapter 7, Obtaining Support from the Organization, gives advice on how an implementation team on the organizational level can support the adoption of RUP in the development projects.

Chapter 8, How to Adopt RUP in Your Project, takes the project view of the adoption. This chapter is also a good starting point for small-scale adoption, where all the process-related work will take place in one or a few development projects.

Chapter 9, Deciding upon Your Process, discusses the topic of RUP tailoring and customization.

Chapter 10, Documenting Your Process, explains how you can physically document (through print publications, Web sites, and so on) the process you have built. The stages that a process documentation undergoes during an implementation are presented.

Chapter 11, A Guide to Successful Mentoring, stems from our firm belief that a process implementation will be faster and more successful when supported by experienced mentors. This chapter describes how such mentorship should be performed.

Appendix A, Experiences from Actual Implementations, provides real-life examples of RUP implementations. Generously, two companies have shared their experiences. In this appendix we summarize their views.

Appendix B, Adding Another Project Management Method to RUP, expands on some details from Chapter 9. Two companies have generously let us show how they—partly—align their project management method with RUP's project management discipline.

Glossary contains a few terms from the RUP terminology and other items that need to be defined for clear understanding.

Acknowledgments

It goes without saying that writing a book involves more people than just the authors. We had the advantage of being close to highly competent colleagues and business contacts with whom we could try ideas during the early phases of the project. Once we had a complete manuscript, we received invaluable help in correcting language, clarifying concepts, and so on.

Special thanks to the following people:

- From the Rational Unified Process business unit: Philippe Kruchten and Gary Pollice, who supported our project from day one. Sigurd Hopen shared the secrets from coming releases of RUP (including PEP and the tools for customizing RUP).
- The team of reviewers: Philippe Kruchten, Gary Pollice, Kurt Bittner, Kelli Houston, Dan Rawsthorne, Barclay Brown, Tony Grout, Axel Josefson, and Chris Soskin, whose feedback made us rethink and improve the content of the book.
- From our local management team: Anders Torelm and Bo Brennermark, who supported our efforts. Thanks to Bo also for reading early drafts and suggesting improvements.

- Our local colleagues who willingly let us try our ideas on them: Mats Rahm, Fredrik Ferm, and Håkan Hellmer, among others.
- From the companies that provided us with the case studies and other material:
  - Boris Karlsson, Volvo IT
  - Kirti Vaidya, Covansys
  - Börje Törnblom and Anders Eriksson, TietoEnator
  - Inger Bergman, Semcon
  - Åke Rundqvist, Ericsson AB
- Among our publishing contacts at Pearson Education and Addison-Wesley: Alannah Eames and Simon Plumtree, who helped us navigate the world of publishing. For taking the project from manuscript to print, thanks to our editor, Mary T. O'Brien; her assistant, Brenda Mulligan; and the production coordinator, Patrick Cash-Peterson. And finally, thanks to Chrysta Meadowbrooke, who gave us invaluable help in correcting the grammar in the book. Without her professionalism and feeling for the written language, our sleepless nights when finalizing the manuscript would have gone on even longer.
- Our new colleague at IBM, Lars Hanses, who helped us find contacts within IBM during the early stages of the IBM acquisition of Rational Software.
- David Reo at the European Software Institute, who offered input and review of the material related to the Balanced IT scorecard.
- Claes Janssen, Swedish psychologist and writer, who gave us input regarding his psychological theory of "the Four Rooms of Change."
- The illustrator, Pia de Veen, who managed to turn the sometimes confused images in our brains into very nice illustrations.

Lotta especially wants to thank:

- Patrik Råberg, my husband and the best man a modern woman can have. Thanks for taking care of Rebecka and Jessica; thanks for all the fruitful discussions and input, mainly on how human beings learn; thanks for cooking all these nice dinners; and thanks for your tremendous support, patience, and love.
- Petra Borthwick, my very best friend and very best supporter in everything I do. Many thanks for spending time and energy helping us with English during the early stages of writing, even before we had the contract.

About the Authors

Stefan Bergström worked for five years at Ericsson AB in different positions as a project and process manager. In November 1998, he joined Rational Software and has been a mentor and an instructor since then, helping several customers in Sweden implement RUP. He now manages the training business at Rational in Scandinavia. Stefan holds an M.Sc. in Mechanical Engineering from The Royal Institute of Technology in Stockholm, Sweden.

Lotta (Ann-Charlotte) Råberg started as a software developer at a consultancy company. Her special interest in visual modeling led her to join Rational Software in May 1995. She has gained solid real-life experiences of RUP through consulting and mentoring at a variety of organizations, helping them succeed with their RUP implementations. She holds an M.Sc. in Computer Science from The Royal Institute of Technology in Stockholm, Sweden.

The authors can be contacted through http://www.adoptingrup.com.

1

How to Adopt RUP in Your Organization

RUP describes how to develop software with good results, quickly and predictably. RUP is much more, but that's its core. Organizations developing software today may want to do so according to the descriptions in RUP. The problem is that because software is complex, the description of how to develop software is complex as well. Consequently, adopting RUP may be tricky.

We won't tell you the details about RUP,[1] but we will help you with many of the practical issues surrounding a RUP adoption within an organization. These practical issues include such things as having good motives for adopting RUP and being able to show a business case for it. You ought to have people assess the current situation, make a sound adoption/implementation plan, and manage the overall RUP adoption. You ought to have RUP mentors who transfer their knowledge about how an applied version

---

1. We recommend you read Kruchten [2000] or Kroll and Kruchten [2003] to learn RUP itself.

of RUP best looks for a particular software development project with a particular set of demands. These are just a few of the practical issues that should be addressed.

Adopting[2] RUP in a whole organization is a major task. The bigger the task, the more carefully it should be handled. It's crucial to take one step at a time, plan that step well, support its implementation carefully, and make adjustments before the next step.

One day your organization will benefit a lot from RUP, that's for sure, but the business benefits will appear only if the adoption succeeds and RUP becomes not a paper-only process but a process in the heart of the software developers (see "When Is RUP Adopted?" later in this chapter). You won't adopt RUP by just reading it (nor by installing it, configuring it, tailoring it, customizing it for that sake). You need to select parts of RUP that address your currently weak areas and practice it. You will learn while practicing, and that practicing *is* the adoption. RUP needs to be experienced to reach your heart.

So how can you adopt RUP within your organization? In Figure 1.1 we present a flow of adoption activities that we recommend you perform if you want RUP to be your future software development process. The flow gives you the whole picture and also sets the scope of this book. The subsequent chapters will explore the details of all activities in this flow. We especially want to highlight Chapter 8, "How to Adopt RUP in Your Project," which we devoted to the single software development project perspective. It is just as good a starting point as this chapter. Which one to choose may depend on how "strategically" you and your organization want to look upon a RUP adoption.

In order to add some structure, we have grouped the adoption activities into three sections. The activities discussed in "Before the Implementation" are normally performed once. If there is a major change in the organization it may, however, be necessary to "restart" the implementation and revisit these activities. The activities mentioned in "During the Implementation" are repeated a number of times throughout the process. We end this chapter with After the Implementation, in which we explore what

---

2. Adoption = assessment + planning + tailoring/customization + implementation (roughly!).

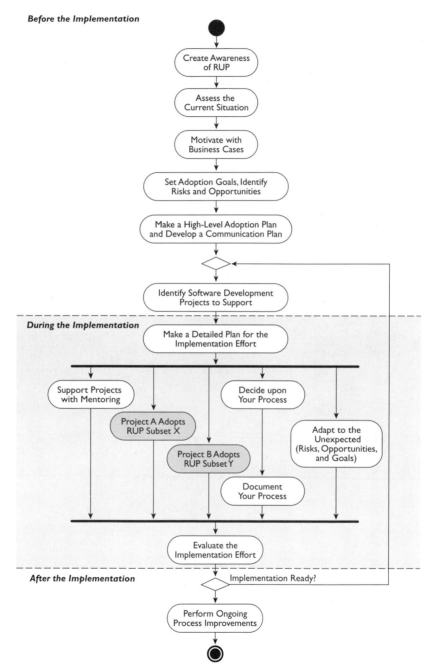

Figure 1.1   *A recommended flow of activities while adopting RUP in a whole organization—a RUP implementation roadmap*

will happen after RUP implementation as well as the subjects of when a RUP implementation is ready and how much RUP you really need.

1.1   Before the Implementation

When implementing RUP in an organization, a number of things have to be done before facing the first software development project. Although the real implementation happens at the project level, supporting activities at the organization level are necessary—mainly to get an overview, keep everything together, and prepare for an effective adoption of RUP without too much overlapping work in the projects. You should also be able to report overall implementation progress. Implementing a process is a major task, so it will take some time and cost some money, making it crucial to show progress along the way.

1.1.1   Create Awareness of RUP

How does a RUP adoption start? Of course, it may vary, but likely some people at your organization recognized a need for improving the way software is developed today. Pretty soon RUP came up as one of the alternatives that would address this. Questions probably arose: "What is RUP?" "What are its benefits?" "What about drawbacks?" "How much does it cost?" "How do we make it happen?"

Whether or not a decision regarding an overall RUP adoption has been made, the first thing that should happen within your organization is to create a general awareness of RUP. At the same time, it is wise to create a general awareness of the future demands your organization will face, demands that may require a change of some kind. Information about RUP may be spread through meetings, seminars, and the intranet, or just informally from one person to another.

In Chapter 2, "The First Meeting with RUP," we have tried to explain RUP without "difficult words" because RUP applies to so many different people—many of them "nontechnical." Scaring people is one of the worst things you can do at this early point in an adoption. Your first challenge will be to convey this *easy* message of what RUP is and to get people interested and a bit curious. Be careful not to complicate things—save all the details and features of RUP for people's second meeting with RUP.

In Chapter 3, "What Is a RUP Project?", we explain RUP in terms of how it looks when applied to project teams that are developing software. Apart from the quick production of good software, what are the characteristics of a RUP project? Chapter 3 requires RUP knowledge but should provide some value to RUP beginners in terms of "painting the picture." People who know about RUP can learn more about when a RUP adoption is ready. The question about how much RUP a project needs to use in order to qualify as a RUP project is a very common one. We try to answer it.

1.1.2 Assess the Current Situation

Fundamental to your RUP adoption is to find out how software is developed today within your organization. What works well? What doesn't work well? About what do people feel most the pain? How does the current development process look? Is there any documentation that people use?

During an *organization assessment*, a small team of assessors interviews a reasonable number of people who hold different roles and belong to different parts of the organization. Information about the current situation is collected. Every area within software development (e.g., requirements, testing, project management, and so on) is investigated and compared with known best practices within the software industry. The assessors also need to understand the business goals of your organization because they are an important input while assessing whether or not current behaviors are effective for the business.

The outcome of the organization assessment is typically an *assessment report* that—after key persons within your organization have agreed upon it—presents the assessment findings and reflects the current software development situation. The assessment findings will be used when deciding whether there is a good reason to adopt RUP at all. If the organization decides to adopt RUP, the findings will also be used when deciding which parts of RUP to adopt and what would be the preferred order. Hence, the assessment report serves as input to both the business case and the adoption plan. Read more in Chapter 4, "Assessing Your Organization."

1.1.3   Motivate with a Business Case

Why should RUP be implemented? Will RUP improve your business? Is there a return on investment (ROI) for adopting RUP? If so, when will the money spent on RUP licenses, training, and mentoring pay for itself? No matter whether the initiative for adopting RUP comes from top management or not, there ought to be a business case for adopting RUP within your organization, and you should make an effort to illustrate this.

The business case motivates management to invest in changing the way software developers work today. In turn, management needs to motivate the software developers for the change to happen and the business case to come through. The business case itself should motivate the software developers, but management also needs to take several other actions, such as investing in RUP training, providing help through RUP mentors, allowing a little extra time, and so on. Read more about this in Chapter 5, "Motivating the RUP Adoption."

1.1.4   Set Adoption Goals, Identify Risks and Opportunities

Making your business case come true will be your top-level goal. But this is a long-term goal that needs to be broken down into a number of short-term, more detailed goals. These short-term goals should help you stay focused and make it possible to follow up the RUP adoption along the way. You should define goals that are relevant for the *organization*, for its *projects*, and for the *individuals* working on those projects. We call these *adoption goals*, which means that the goals should connect to the RUP adoption. As an example, probably the most important project goal would be "Ensure that every project that uses RUP succeeds." Read more about this goal and others in Chapter 6, "Planning the RUP Adoption."

When heading for the defined goals, bad things or good things may happen within the organization or any of its projects. Many dangers likely lie in wait during a RUP adoption, most of them related to human factors or business changes of any kind. You should maintain a *risk list* and plan for appropriate actions in case any of your fears are confirmed. But don't focus on the negative only! Also watch out for positive things and take advantage of all *opportunities* from the RUP adoption's point of view. Maybe a project "perfect for RUP" suddenly begins, or an external consultant experienced in RUP is hired as the software architect in department A. Take advantage of such opportunities and make them part of your RUP adoption!

1.1.5 Make a High-Level Adoption Plan and Develop a Communication Plan

The next step is to put your adoption goals into an adoption plan and start defining major activities that will take you toward these goals and eventually make the business case come true. The assessment findings are the most important input, but identified risks and opportunities may also be reflected in some activities. But just as in modern iterative software development (as described in RUP), making an excessively detailed plan early in the process is a trap. Things *will* happen that will cause you to change your plan. However, a high-level, rough plan that covers the whole adoption effort is needed in order to communicate how the adoption is to proceed. Also, the implementation team members must not lose focus or speed; they have to stick to long-term goals and a long-term time schedule. Read more in Chapter 6, "Planning the RUP Adoption," which also brings up the important topic of continuously communicating to people what is happening throughout the RUP adoption.

1.1.6 Identify Software Development Projects to Support (Pilot Projects)

We have stated that the real implementation of RUP happens on the project level, which means that the real implementation of RUP *starts* within the first supported software development projects. This means that it is not so good to start a RUP adoption during a period of time when no new projects are planned to begin. Of course, you may choose to adopt RUP for maintenance of previously released software, but you should also save your strengths for future projects that develop new software.

When making a considerable change, it is very important to get off to a good start. Therefore, the first supported projects are critical. These first supported projects are often called *RUP pilot projects* to indicate that they are the first ones to try using RUP within the organization's official RUP adoption effort. (Some projects might have applied parts of RUP "on their own" before.) It is important that the first projects are suitable, that RUP is relevant for them, and that they succeed. It is also good if the project's focus is fairly typical within the organization so that the RUP experiences can be reused in future projects. Read more about pilot projects and other implementation strategies in Chapter 6, "Planning the RUP Adoption."

1.2   During the Implementation

At this point, the actual implementation has now started, and a number of software development projects are adopting RUP. These projects are getting help from RUP mentors who assist each project manager with detailed plans for the RUP implementation and support the projects on all RUP-related issues.

Apart from supporting more and more projects, some activities on the organization level will be repeated several times during the implementation. Your organizational process, that is, the collected works of proven parts of RUP, is continuously built up as experiences are made within projects and shared with others. You will follow up the progress of the implementation, communicate to the whole organization what is happening, and watch for things that may cause the plans to change.

1.2.1   Make a Detailed Plan for the Implementation Effort

As soon as software development projects that are to implement RUP have been identified, it is possible to detail the high-level adoption plan.[3] The identified projects will have different requirements regarding process and tools that impact the implementation activities. Which project will explore which parts of the process? Which RUP subsets will require the most support, and how is that support best given? What training and mentoring is needed and when?

The RUP implementation will affect each project's software development plan as well as the iteration plans. Among the other planned project activities, you will find RUP-related activities—RUP training, RUP workshops,

---

3. Those of you familiar with RUP can compare RUP projects that have their high-level project plan in the software development plan and their detailed project plan in the iterations plans.

RUP reviews, and the RUP artifacts that are expected as deliverables. Each project will also have a development case, explaining exactly which RUP subset is used and what to do within the areas where RUP is not yet adopted.

But the detailed RUP implementation planning activities should not be distributed to the projects only. Sometimes synergies may arise. For example, the start-up support that each project needs may be similar, and the design of that support could be coordinated. Perhaps people need to attend a RUP course more or less at the same time; such training could be arranged cost effectively. The detailed plan on the organization level is necessary in order to keep things together and to distribute acquired RUP support resources (mentors) between the projects. Read more in Chapter 7, "Obtaining Support from the Organization."

1.2.2   Support Projects with Mentoring (Among Other Things)

This is a particularly crucial part of the implementation. Your organization should provide support to the software development projects that will adopt RUP.

Mainly the support should consist of mentoring; that is, a RUP mentor should be made available in order to help with the projects adopting RUP. The RUP mentor helps by selecting appropriate parts of RUP to start with, showing team members how to use these parts of RUP, and showing them how to customize these parts if necessary in order for RUP to apply better and be really useful. The RUP mentor may run workshops and perform reviews. The value of the mentor helping people with the change in general should not be underestimated (see Figure 1.2). Read more in Chapter 11, "A Guide to Successful Mentoring."

Apart from mentoring, project team members need help with training; they need to know which courses people in various roles should take as well as when it is possible to enroll. This kind of help is important because it lets the team members stay focused on the software they should develop. Remember, every project team adopting RUP needs to succeed— everything else would be bad for the RUP adoption.

The project teams also need assistance with tools. Your organization should support RUP with appropriate development tools that automate

Figure 1.2   *A RUP mentor ensures the success of a RUP adoption by transferring knowledge and facilitating change.*

and simplify parts of the work. The tools need to be integrated with the process used, and your organization should help projects with guidelines for this as well as basic things like installation, setup, upgrades, and so on.

As a final point, the team members should be supported in their obligations[4] of sharing their experiences of RUP. For example, the group that supports the RUP adoption overall will collect valuable material (the tailored process, examples, detailed guidelines, and so on) to become part of the organizational process. Read more in Chapter 7, "Obtaining Support from the Organization."

---

4. The adoption effort will surely benefit from this. However, there might be cases when this is not possible or even allowed due to confidentiality issues, lack of time, and so on.

1.2.3 Software Projects Adopt Particular RUP Subsets

This is where the real RUP adoption takes place, within software development projects! From the development project team's point of view, adopting RUP encompasses the following four steps.

1. Assess your project.
2. Select a subset from RUP and plan the implementation of that subset.
3. Run your project and get support on RUP.
4. Share RUP experiences with people from other projects.

These steps will be repeated for each development project that is part of the overall implementation that is, another project might select a different subset from RUP to implement. Read more in Chapter 8, "How to Adopt RUP in Your Project."

We give you guidelines on how to support a project in the best possible way in Chapter 7, "Obtaining Support from the Organization," and Chapter 11, "A Guide to Successful Mentoring." Remember, without successful running of "real" software development projects where RUP is adopted, no successful RUP implementation will ever take place.

1.2.4 Decide upon Your Process and Document It

When software development project teams adopt RUP, they will decide how to use RUP. At the same time, your organization's way to use RUP will be decided! These decisions need to be documented in one way or another. The projects adopting RUP will produce valuable material in the form of guidelines, checklists, templates, and so on that should be harvested and collected at the organization level and in this way shared with all people within your organization. Also, real project artifacts may be collected, and upcoming projects can reuse appropriate parts.

But shouldn't the intended detailed process to follow be in place when projects start? Not necessarily. At the start of the first RUP pilot projects there will be available, at most, high-level recommendations,[5] for example,

---

5. This you may call an initially customized organizational process, but note that the customization at this point in time is very, very rough and course grained, such as "Follow requirements as described in RUP," "Perform test the old way," "Use the old project management method but add iteration plans from RUP," and "Bring in the J2EE RUP plug-in."

"Perform requirements capture as described in RUP." After the first projects there will be some material available for reuse, such as examples of use case models and perhaps a document of common use case modeling guidelines that all projects have been using. But the final, detailed process for a particular project always needs to be defined in the project itself.

Predicting what would be a perfect process up front does not work. We have seen such initiatives going on for months at some organization, only to find out that none of the nice ideas ever got implemented. Of course, you should have some basic ideas of how an appropriate process may look for a particular project, but you decide upon the detailed process along the way. Project team members should start doing their job (develop software) as soon as possible and not be delayed by process issues. In cases when there is a need for tailoring/customization of the process, this is performed very close to the real work. Typically a process engineer (RUP mentor) writes down what has proven to be a working process among the project team members and finds a good way to merge or insert this into existing RUP activities. In this way the process engineer harvests working processes from the projects, rather than making up things for the team members to try.

In Chapter 9, "Deciding upon Your Process," we discuss various ways to determine what your process should be. In Chapter 10, "Documenting Your Process," we talk about how it could be documented.

1.2.5   Adapt to the Unexpected (Handle Risks, Opportunities, and Goals)

During the implementation effort, the risk list created earlier needs to be revisited and reassessed. Some of the initial risks now have been taken care of, or they may have ceased to be of concern. New risks usually arise. The main issue is to be continuously aware of the risks. It is not enough just to list the risks—evaluate their probability and consequences, and develop and execute plans for how to actively reduce the risks throughout the course of the project. Also, you should continuously keep an eye open for new opportunities within the organization that may be beneficial for the RUP adoption to address.

Just as changes in the world around you (and yes, there will be some changes) will cause new risks or opportunities, you will need to investigate how the changes will affect your goals for the RUP adoption. For example, if you had a goal like "The communication between department A and B shall be improved," a reorganization might have made it irrelevant. Even if there is no need to change the goals, it might be possible to further detail some of the original goals because you know more at this stage, after one or more projects have adopted RUP.

1.2.6 Evaluate the Implementation Effort

When one or more software development projects have been finished (or at some other suitable point in time), it is important to evaluate the results. The team members who have adopted and tried RUP have gained experiences and will have opinions on what parts of the process have been particularly useful and what parts have been hard to apply without some customization. Moreover, the team members will have opinions regarding the support they have been given in terms of training, mentoring, tools, and so on.

It is not uncommon that the management wants to see some results from the implementation before committing resources and money to the next phase. If you have chosen a more formal method of following up the capability of the organization, this is the time to do such a follow-up. If no formal method will be used, you should at least distribute a questionnaire in order to collect people's views on the RUP-based process, how well the RUP adoption proceeded, whether they believe things are better now than before, and so on. Read more in "Following Up the Business Case and People's Attitudes" section in Chapter 5.

Use the evaluations as a source of information for finding reasons to adjust your adoption goals and your implementation plans. And, of course, the results of the evaluations should be communicated to everyone in the organization. People in the organization want to know how the implementation proceeds and whether it is successful!

1.3   After the Implementation

Is there really such a phase as *after* the implementation? Frankly, looking at RUP and everything in it, as well as considering all the employees who comprise organizations, so far we haven't encountered an organization whose RUP implementation can be regarded as complete. Either there are more parts of RUP that can be implemented or there are more parts of the organization that can adopt RUP. But are these the criteria for judging whether the implementation is complete?

Some organizations have been running special RUP implementation projects for a couple of years and have now ended these projects. Does this mean they have completed their implementation of RUP? What are these organizations doing with RUP now?

1.3.1   When Is the Implementation Done?

First answer: never. Second answer: when the adoption goals have been reached. Third answer: when you decide that it is. Even if not all goals have been reached and not all parts of RUP have been implemented, the commitment from the management will stretch for a certain time and eventually come to an end. In a sense, the implementation of RUP is then done. Your high-level plan has an end date, and when passing that date you know what you accomplished.

Our belief is that an organization has the strength and patience to run an implementation of RUP for, at the most, three or four years. After that, RUP and its implementation *won't get anymore special attention.* This may be a criterion for determining whether an implementation is done—no more allocation of additional RUP implementation resources to projects, no more extra "energy." But as long as there are software development projects, the process will evolve. Issues with RUP and tools will be handled within the projects as normal process and method matters, which we recommend be supported by an established Process and Tool Support Center (described later in this chapter).

When Is RUP Adopted? A process is fully implemented when everyone in your organization understands the fundamental principles behind the process and how to base decisions on those principles—actually, when everyone puts the principles into practice on a daily basis. In contrast, if a minor group decides upon an intended process and makes its documentation available all over, this will not automatically change the behavior in your organization. It is important to understand why change happens and how to achieve changes in the ways individuals in an organization perform their work.

The employees should know where to seek information about how to perform work, how to set the process into practice. The ways a task is performed in different places in the organization do not have to be identical. However, they should be similar, based on the same principles. We have seen too many examples of organizations that said they use RUP (mainly based on the fact that the management team made the decision to use RUP in the development), but when it came to practice, to the ways people performed their tasks, it became obvious that RUP was not used coherently and sometimes not even properly.

To simplify the discussion, we describe two (extreme) levels of awareness of the process among the employees.

- *Paper-only process*: Creating documents and Web pages or changing the tree browser in RUP does not implement the process in the organization. People will not start to work in a new way just because you write a few documents. In our experiences, organizations that chose to complete their own variants of RUP before starting RUP projects have often ended up with wonderful Web sites that very few people in the organizations use. Why? Because the practitioners do not see the process as their own, or they do not trust it to work (because they have not seen examples of it working!).
- *Process in the hearts of the employees*: In order for people to adopt the process and make it their own, they need to see personal benefits from it as well as benefits for the organization. They also want to be involved in defining what parts of the process to use. A team consists of individuals with individual needs. The first step in creating awareness of the change is to involve as many people as possible in the assessment. The best way to reduce skepticism is to prove that the process works and helps the organization as well as the individuals—and this can be proven only during real projects. If the skeptic is involved in a successful project using RUP, it will be hard for him or her to criticize the process. So if you encounter a really stubborn skeptic, make him or her responsible for parts of the process. Involvement is key to buy-in.

In order for the process to become implemented, we need to change the ways people act. If the employees are given opportunities to try parts of the new process and influence how it is applied, they will adopt it faster. Decisions about the process, documentation, and so on are important, but decisions about how to change the behavior in the organization and how the people in it act are even more important.

Do not complete a tailored or customized version of RUP before starting the implementation. Following this simple rule is a strategic decision; we even think it is vital for the success of implementations. So when should the tailored version be completed? To achieve a configuration that fits the organization as well as possible, the configuration needs to be done in parallel with one or more actual development (pilot) projects.

How Much RUP Do You Need? Finally, we need to say that adopting RUP shouldn't be an end in itself. What you do need is to develop good software quickly and predictably. If you do that successfully already, you should be really careful about changing your current process. There is no point in changing something that works! You should start initiatives of adopting RUP only if you have problems with your current process or if you are pretty sure that your current process will not work due to some new demands your software development teams will be facing.

It's another question—and actually a pretty uninteresting one compared to what you need in order to be successful—but if you would like to know how much RUP you need in order to call your project a RUP project, read more in Chapter 3, "What Is a RUP Project?".

1.3.2   Perform Ongoing Process Improvements

What about a few years from now? The implementation will be done, but the world around you will change. The technology and tools will evolve and RUP will be updated; the demands on your system might be altered. Your process needs to follow, or you will fall behind. Who is responsible for the maintenance[6] of your organization's RUP-based process? Who is responsible for handling the upgrades of the supporting tools? It is important to discuss during the implementation the *ownership* of the process and tools. We recommend that you establish a Process and Tool Support Center (see Figure 1.3).

---

6. By the way, ease of maintenance should be a key concern for any RUP customization.

This Process and Tool Support Center (or team or department, if you like) will be responsible for managing and encouraging ongoing process improvements within the organization. If a special implementation project team (see Chapter 7, "Obtaining Support from the Organization") handled the implementation, the Process and Tool Support Center takes over and performs more or less the same daily tasks. The center will support projects with mentors performing workshops, reviews, tool installations, and so on; it will adjust your organization's RUP-based process to the changing needs of the organization; and it will educate new employees in the basics of your application of RUP as well as provide skills training in RUP.

Without ongoing process improvement, the organization's process will "get out of sync" with the way people perform work—just as when the system documentation gets out of sync with the code after a few updates and upgrades (which will never happen if the team lives and works in the spirit of RUP, of course). So once you've started implementing RUP, you will never escape from being aware of your software engineering process!

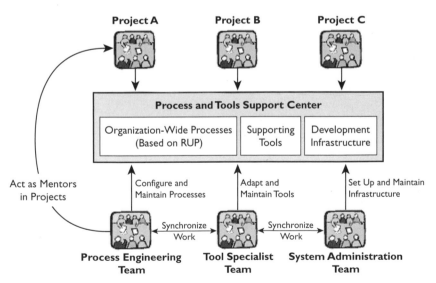

Figure 1.3 *The Process and Tool Support Center helps software development project teams apply RUP and the recommended tools.*

1.4   Conclusion

When introducing RUP in an organization, several activities need to be performed. Before the actual implementation starts, you should create a general awareness of what RUP is, what the future demands on the software development in your organization are, and the reasons for changing the current way of working. In fact, you need to thoroughly assess your organization to learn about the current situation. What are your strengths, and what are your weaknesses? What needs to be done, and which of today's procedures fits the future demands? You need to create a high-level plan of the work to come, which may well last a few years. The implementation cannot start until you have identified a first project to try out the new process.

During the implementation, this project and maybe a few more need to get supported by the organization, which will provide mentoring and additional resources. In turn, the project team members share their adaptation and their experiences with the organization as a whole. More and more project teams will start to adopt RUP; the organizational adaptation will grow and become more and more precise and supportive. One day you will have reached your goals with the implementation.

After the implementation is completed, you need to make sure that the organization keeps the process updated to reflect changes in the organization and the environment. This will lead to what is often called ongoing process improvements.

In the next chapter, we will remind you of the basic concepts in RUP and how to relate to it before starting to discuss the adoption of RUP in more detail.

2

The First Meeting with RUP

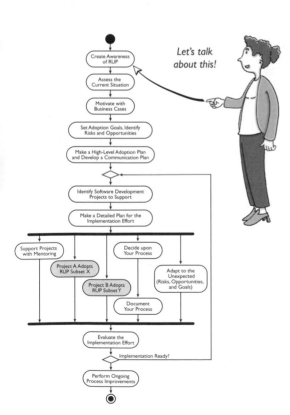

Let's talk about this!

Within every company and every organization, a number of business processes run on a day-to-day basis. These processes are more or less obvious to us as processes, because processes have a clear *start*, a clear *end*, and a number of well-defined *steps in between*.

One process that should be very clear for a merchandise company is the *order process*. This process is likely to start with a call from a customer. A sales administrator takes the call and makes a note about what was ordered, who ordered it, and where to send the item. The sales administrator hands the request to somebody in the warehouse, who checks whether the item is in stock. If so, the item is sent to the customer. A finance administrator is notified and sends an invoice.

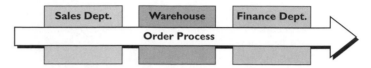

Figure 2.1   *An order process consists of activities from different departments.*

As in all business processes, a number of individuals are involved in the order process. These individuals have responsibilities that make them perform some activities. Together these activities make up the order process (see Figure 2.1). If the company is fairly large, its executive managers probably decided to invest in a supporting computer system at some point. The reasoning behind their decision most likely involved a desire to make the order process more efficient so that the same number of people could handle even more orders and still get everything right.

In companies and organizations doing programming, or to be precise, building computer systems, there is probably one business process known as the order process. But there is also a quite important process known as the *software engineering process* (or *software development process*)—a business process that covers everyone and everything involved when building software, that is, computer systems. It might feel strange viewing the sometimes chaotic and complex world of programming as a business process, but that is what it is. Figure 2.2 shows how some of the activities that make up this kind of process relate to each other.

The software engineering process differs a lot from organization to organization. Depending on who has been involved historically and what kinds of systems have been built so far, the established ways of working will differ. Over time a number of practices evolve within a company, which newcomers need to learn in order to function in a software development team. Presumably the "old-timers" sit down with newcomers and explain the basics, but it will likely take quite a long time until newly hired people or consultants understand how things work and can become fully productive.

Let us revisit the order process. If, for instance, a new sales administrator has been appointed recently, the old sales administrator may have written

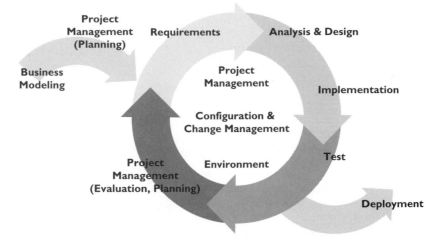

Figure 2.2 *The software engineering process consists of activities from different competence areas (disciplines).*

some notes in order to help the new sales administrator in his or her work. These notes may be in the form of a bulleted list on what actions to take when a customer calls, just in case one forgets what to do at that point. Perhaps also the person in the warehouse has written down something regarding how to handle tricky orders. In this way the order process not only exists as a routine but also is *documented*—fragmented, of course, but still documented.

Software engineering processes of companies may also be more or less documented, but they are most likely even more fragmented than an order process because of the difficulty in discovering routines within the creative world of software engineering. The routines, if discovered at all, probably appear as a less critical issue. It is more important to come up with good technical ideas that are necessary to actually get the software in place at all. The task of recognizing and establishing routines gets low priority, which is reasonable because the routines and processes themselves are typically not part of the business drivers of a software development company.

However, some work has been done focusing on the software engineering process itself. RUP is a documentation of a software engineering process. Whose software engineering process? Well, everybody's and nobody's. RUP is a process framework,[1] a well-recognized and exhaustive framework with *a lot of content*. Putting it this way, there is probably no company in the world that would follow and work according to *all* descriptions found in RUP. But if a company follows the parts of RUP that *are* suitable for it, that company will work in a proper way, following the guidance and advice from other experienced software developers and their ideas of the best way to produce software. Is this guidance and advice strange or perhaps surprising? No, most software people regard the advice as common sense and are often surprised that RUP is "nothing new."

2.1   Packaged Common Sense

The common sense of an experienced software project manager, a veteran software acquirer, a software testing professional, a software architect, a software developer—all the common sense of people involved in software engineering has been collected, documented, and stored in one place, one package. Plain text as well as numerous graphs and illustrations have been used in RUP to describe the different aspects of software development. The content for each topic varies, but the structure and organization are the same. Also, the vocabulary is uniform in the sense that the same word or concept always has the same meaning regardless of the surrounding contents.

What kind of content can be found in RUP? Well, the scope is "how to develop software,"[2] and the advice given should apply to many people at various companies and organizations. This means that the descriptions cannot be too specific. Everything that is special and more or less unique to a certain company or organization has been removed. Also, everything that is very specific for a particular kind of product or system has been removed—or at least lifted from the mainstream advice. For example, RUP does not tell you things like "If you expect to have 300 simulta-

---

1. Framework: "A structure for supporting or enclosing something else, especially a skeletal support used as the basis for something being constructed" or "A set of assumptions, concepts, values, and practices that constitutes a way of viewing reality" (http://www.yourdictionary.com/ahd/f/f0293800.html).
2. Includes maintaining and configuring software.

neous users ordering books through an intended Web application, you should use the X structure in your design and use the CORBA Y product for your communication with the database." Instead, RUP says things like "Analyze how many simultaneous users you are going to have," "Consider whether a thin-client approach or a thick-client approach best suits your needs," and "Determine which third-party products are going to be part of your system."

For each topic, RUP provides guidance about what steps need to be taken and what decisions need to be made. RUP reminds you: "Have you thought about this and this?" and "When you have this situation, you can select between these alternatives." Still, *you* need to make the decisions. *Your* decisions create *your* system!

2.2   Presented through a Product

The package of "documented common sense" is also a commercially available product, developed and maintained by IBM Rational Software. An updated RUP version is released frequently, which means that you can be assured that RUP does not get old-fashioned or unusable. Instead, it is kept up-to-date with the latest technology and practices. Still, the heart of RUP has remained stable for some years now, and there are many indications that the fundamental terminology and working methods in RUP will last. The main idea behind RUP is to enable companies to focus on building systems rather than building and maintaining the *process* for building systems.

RUP is more than just a "way of thinking" or a "method" presented in a book; it is a framework for a software development process. IBM Rational Software has packaged this framework into a product so that RUP can be used across the world in a common although not identical way. RUP is widespread and has been for quite some time. Many RUP users have shared what they need and want from RUP, as well as what has worked and what hasn't been working. This has resulted in long lists of relevant improvements in order to make RUP increasingly useful. This, combined with the ideas from many "thought leaders,"[3] as well as the hard work of

---

3. Grady Booch, Ivar Jacobson, Bran Selic, Philippe Kruchten, and many more.

the RUP product development team editing all the details, has lead to a continuously improved product.

2.2.1   What Is the RUP Product?

Physically, the RUP documentation is placed on a CD-ROM (or it can be downloaded via the Internet). By opening the RUP start page in an Internet browser, you can surf around and reach everything. All pages can also be installed on your personal computer or placed on a server at your company so people can reach them via the intranet.

RUP can be compared to an online software engineering encyclopedia. This means that you can look up various subjects and learn about them. The subjects, which are explained in words and in pictures, also contain links to other related subjects. If printed out, they would fill several thousands of pages. Hence, a lot of information is presented, and a good structure as well as good search functions come in handy. Figure 2.3 shows the most recognized graph describing RUP.

What does RUP *not* allow you to do? You cannot store anything in RUP. For this you use the ordinary file system on a computer or, better, a configura-

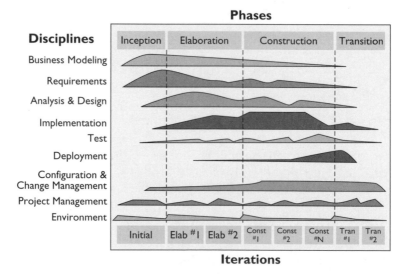

Figure 2.3   *This picture has become a logo for the RUP product. It is the starting point for the first level of navigation in RUP.*

tion management tool. You cannot draw in RUP. The drawing language suggested by RUP is the Unified Modeling Language (UML), which is a standard maintained by the Object Management Group (OMG; refer to http://www.omg.org/uml). For drawing UML models you need a special UML modeling tool.

What *can* you do? You can search for information on how to develop software. The information you'll find is linked in a logical way to other information you might need. Best of all, it is possible to find information based on what *role* (see the next subsection) you are to perform in a project. You can also use the extra RUP tools, which enable you to configure and change the standard appearance of RUP. These tools—RUP Builder, RUP Organizer, among others—will be described in more detail in Chapter 10.

2.2.2   The Structure of RUP

The structure of the RUP documentation reflects how an actual development project is planned and organized. When building software, you basically need two things: a number of skilled *people* and some *time*. These are key necessities for a project. These are also key issues for the structure of RUP, which must not only focus on supporting the people doing the work but also express when (in which order) the work shall be done. The same framework for process documentation should be valuable for small, short-term projects as well as for large, long-term ones.

The people within a project team will turn to RUP in order to get support for their day-to-day work. It should be easy to trace down to the parts of the RUP documentation that are relevant for each individual. The first thing for people to learn is in which *discipline* (or competence area) they will be active.

Different people have different skills. The various skills and areas of concern involved when building software have been grouped into nine disciplines in RUP: Business Modeling,[4] Requirements, Analysis & Design, Implementation, Deployment, Test, Project Management, Configuration & Change

---

4. Not part of the RUP base but recommended for many organizations.

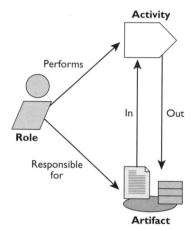

Figure 2.4   *The concepts of role, activity, and artifact are central for the RUP notation. A role performs an activity to produce or update an artifact. While doing this the role may use other previously produced artifacts as input.*

Management, and Environment. The disciplines are visible on the left side in Figure 2.3.

Within the documentation for each discipline, people will find one or more *roles* they could play during the project. Each role has a number of *activities* to be performed, where each activity has detailed and supportive step-by-step descriptions. When performing an activity, a number of *artifacts* (or work products, e.g., documents, models, pieces of code) will be produced. The person who holds the related role will be responsible for these artifacts during the project (see Figure 2.4).

How do people relate to roles? A role defines a certain responsibility in a project. A person in the project can assume that responsibility and "play the role." Typically, in a small project one person may assume the responsibilities of more than one role, and in larger projects a team of people may take responsibility for one specific role (e.g., an architecture team may play the role of software architect). In this way people get support from RUP, and the common sense mentioned above mostly materializes within activity descriptions as well as in guidelines for artifacts.

However, the documentation retrieved via the disciplines does not tell you much about time. It says nothing about *when* to perform an activity. It says nothing about to what extent a certain artifact must be finished before handing it over to a project member skilled in another discipline. For this the *phases* of RUP are needed.

One option would have been to document everything that has to do with time planning within the Project Management discipline. But since the time aspect is so important for RUP, especially when determining *in which order* a system should be built, certain aspects regarding time planning appear all the way up to the top-level structure of RUP.

All projects developed according to RUP are divided into four phases: Inception, Elaboration, Construction, and Transition. (For explanation of what happens in each phase, refer to RUP or to Examples of the New Language, below.) Regardless of how small or how big the development effort is, the phases are always the same. How long a phase needs to be depends on how long it will take until the *milestone* ending the phase can be passed. It is also necessary to determine the number of *iterations* needed within each phase in order to maintain good control with the development. RUP documentation describes the objectives and essential activities of each phase. Figure 2.3 shows which disciplines are active during each phase and to what extent a specific discipline is active in relation to other disciplines.

RUP also describes the *criteria* that must be met and the *artifacts* that must be produced in order to pass the milestone ending each phase. It is important to understand that artifacts do not always have to be 100% complete in order to "count" at a certain milestone. For example, a master test plan may be only 10% complete at the end of Inception and 90% complete at the end of Elaboration. This is actually one of the key characteristics of iterative development.

Every project team needs to plan each of its iterations in detail in terms of the actual requirements, risks, and so on. However, RUP contains examples of typical iteration plans for each phase to use as starting points (see Figure 2.5).

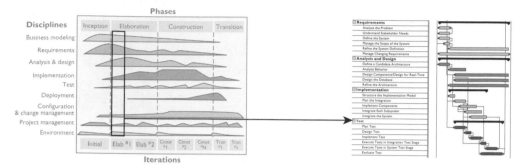

Figure 2.5   *RUP offers sample iteration plans defined for each phase.*

In summary, using disciplines as a starting point helps you find documentation on who will do something (role), how something should be done (activity), and what this something is (artifact). Tracing down via phases helps you find documentation on when to perform activities, when the work with a certain artifact shall be started, and when the work should be completed to a certain state or finalized.

2.3   Knowledge Base

RUP is a big knowledge base containing the know-how from hundreds of software engineering specialists. Through the years it has grown in breadth and now covers the entire software lifecycle, that is, all development activities from the initial idea of building a system to the day the system is phased out for good. Over time the RUP knowledge base has also grown in depth, in the sense that activity descriptions, guidelines, tool mentors, and similar items have become more detailed and therefore more supportive.

Still, when it comes to breadth as well as depth, the documentation needs to be kept on a *generally applicable, universal level*. In order to fit almost every development project, the documentation must be neither too specific nor too specialized. RUP as a framework is described in a way that makes it possible to create a suitable process for any imaginable project (see Figure 2.6).

Figure 2.6   *You may need to tailor and/or customize RUP in order to make it "fit" within your organization.*

But don't panic—more specialized documentation is also available, and more is to come. You can, for example, find more specific support on how to design and code on certain development platforms (Integrated Development Environment, or IDE) from specific vendors. (The technique for extending RUP is known as *RUP plug-ins*; see Chapter 9, "Deciding Upon Your Process.")

However, this is not enough. The recommendation is that every company should *expand RUP with its own unique knowledge*. Many companies rely on the specialized expertise of their employees as their most significant asset. Inspired by RUP, employees can start documenting their know-how.

This can be done in various ways. For example, one method is to collect project artifacts and make them accessible as examples for everybody in the organization. Project-specific guidelines are especially valuable because they express general rules, tips, and tricks that the project team decided to follow, for example, during design work. Another way is to specialize various RUP activities by rewriting them (or, rather, commenting on them) in light of the special, unique situation at a company. In this way an activity description gets more "down to earth," becomes very easy to follow, and is very supportive. The scope for free interpretation is reduced, and everyone does things in very similar ways.

2.4   Common Language

When a company starts using RUP, things will happen to the language used among its employees. *A new language will be established.* The RUP terminology will mix with current terminology used within the company. Some terms and concepts will be completely new. Some terms may exist within the company today, but with RUP their true meaning may get slightly changed or sometimes changed considerably. Some terms—as a matter of fact, a lot of terms—will stay intact. Remember that RUP affects only the "how to" language. The terms from the company problem domain, terms related to what *kinds* of systems are being built, will stay the same.

After a while a new common language will develop among different roles in the organization. This has a lot of benefits, because speaking the same language promotes efficient communication and enables people to focus completely on problems to be solved and systems to be built.

2.5   Examples of the New Language

What is the new common language of RUP? A number of terms and concepts may be regarded as "typical RUP": *iterations, risks, controlled iterative development, architecture,* the phases of RUP (*Inception, Elaboration, Construction,* and *Transition*), and all the *models,* especially the one with *use cases.*

In order to understand what RUP is, you need to have a basic understanding of at least these terms and concepts. To feel comfortable when reading the rest of the book, the same basic understanding should be enough. If you want a deeper understanding of all the RUP terminology, please refer to the book *The Rational Unified Process: An Introduction, Third Edition* by Philippe Kruchten [2003] or to the RUP product itself, particularly its glossary of the various "concept" pages.

Figure 2.7   *If people speaking about the same thing use different language, they are likely to misunderstand each other.*

A RUP project proceeds by planning and carrying out a number of *iterations* one after another. An iteration in RUP includes work from more or less all of the nine RUP disciplines (Requirements, Analysis & Design, Implementation, Test, and so on). Every iteration (except perhaps the very first one) results in code. This code could and should be tested right away. The system evolves iteratively, and therefore we say RUP is an *iterative process*.

It is important to point out the fact that RUP is a *controlled iterative process*. Iterations do not just happen; instead they are carefully planned to handle one or more identified *risks*. A risk may be anything that could hinder or delay a project team from successfully building valuable software. RUP promotes risk reduction in the sense that all known risks should be resolved as soon as possible in a project. The awareness of the risks influences the planning of the project. RUP means *risk-driven development*, and the particular technical risks decide in what order to build the increments of the system.

Most technical risks regard the *architecture*. By defining and validating[5] an appropriate architecture for the system, you can solve the technical risks. An architecture according to RUP encompasses all significant decisions about the organization of a software system. (A RUP architecture is more than a network of computers; actually, it is more about software than hardware.) This may be compared with architectural plans for buildings in that architectural plans by no means are the houses themselves nor even their foundations or iron girders. Instead, an architectural plan for a building includes numerous drawings and models showing different aspects of exteriors, interiors, ventilation, piping, and so on. The architect explains his or her ideas regarding the building's characteristics and how it will look to the people who will actually build the building. The same applies for software architects and their software architecture. Architecture is important for RUP, and we say that RUP is *architecture-centric*. The RUP *Elaboration* phase is devoted mainly to architecture.

Also, the iterations are controlled in the sense that they are *time-boxed*. Iterations have an end date, and by that date an iteration assessment is performed. Information about the lessons learned, the results so far, new risks, the quality of the planning itself, and so on is collected in order to plan the work in the next iteration the best possible way.

Without getting into too much detail on the RUP phases, which are *not* time-boxed, *Inception* can be finished when there is a basic understanding of the scope of the development. *Elaboration* can be finished when a good-enough technical solution (architecture) has been established. *Construction* can be finished when a working, fully scoped system has been built. *Transition* can be finished when the system has its release and is handed over, together with supporting documentation, to the people who will own and maintain the system from that point onward.

---

5. That is, tried in code! (A paper-only architecture is *not* enough.)

Finally, RUP implies the use of a lot of *models*, and RUP may therefore be described as a *model-driven process*. Within RUP you find business models of various kinds, a use case model, an analysis model, a design model, a data model, and an implementation model. A model is a complete description of a software system from some viewpoint. For example, an analysis model is a complete description of a system in terms of an object-oriented ideal design independent of the technical solution. An implementation model for the same system has *the same scope* as the analysis model but describes the system through corresponding code. A use case model is a complete description of a system's functional requirements in terms of use cases.

Use cases define sequences of activities, including variants, that a system may perform when interacting with its *actors* in order to give them something of value. Actors are humans or external systems that the system will interact with the day it is up and running. We utilize use cases when describing what the system to be built will do. One of the advantages of use cases is that they mainly are described in natural language, which means that nearly *anyone* can understand them and ask for changes when they seem to catch the wrong ideas. The use cases play a key role in RUP, and because use cases are a kind of "driving engine" within RUP, we say that RUP is *use case driven*.[6] The content of iterations is expressed not only by which risks will be solved but also by which use cases (or parts of use cases) will be described, designed, coded, and tested. RUP also defines that the creation of other models, such as design models, as well as test artifacts should be influenced by the use cases.

2.6   A Way to Help Project Teams Develop Products More Efficiently

The ultimate purpose of RUP is to help project teams develop software projects more efficiently and reliably. By using RUP, software development will be more predictable, more precise, more qualitative, and safer. As a result, companies that depend on RUP in their software development will generally have high productivity and offer high-quality products.

---

6. Read more in *Use Case Modeling* [Bittner and Spence 2003].

Using RUP will help companies create more relevant and trustworthy documentation. This is invaluable when maintaining and evolving new generations of a system. This is also a key condition for avoiding too much dependency on individuals, who seldom stay at the same company for very long. Or worse, some people disappear after the first release because they were hired as consultants.

The good news is that the advantages of using RUP appear quickly. Project teams that have not fulfilled their goals even when using RUP will at least come closer to them than if RUP had not been used. Rudimentary requirements management is better than no requirements management at all. Improved communication between different groups within an organization is a step forward.

The computer business is a relatively immature industry compared with, for instance, the car manufacturing industry. Today's cars are efficiently built in a highly automated process. But imagine what it was like building a car in 1920. Back then, building a car was a craft—it took a very long time, and almost certainly all the pieces didn't fit together the first time. There was no reuse of standard platforms and not so many extra features. By beginning to use a process, the software industry takes the first step toward becoming as professional as other established industries.

2.7   Conclusion

RUP consists mostly of common sense—a lot of it! The specific structure of RUP, oriented around the three basic concepts of role, activity, and artifact, makes it easy to find knowledge that suits your needs when developing software. Furthermore, RUP defines a common language among practitioners that helps you improve teamwork and communication. RUP will help you develop good software quickly. Continuing the spirit of RUP by collecting your own unique experiences from software development is a good habit.

In the next chapter, we will answer common questions about RUP and discuss how running a project according to RUP can look.

3

What Is a RUP Project?

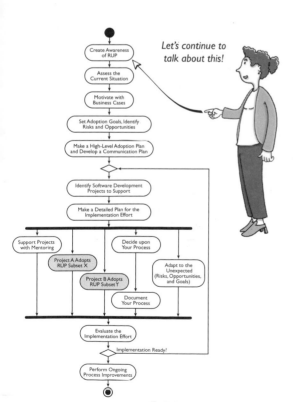

Let's continue to talk about this!

What makes a project a RUP project? Yes, it is a project that uses RUP to some extent, but what apart from that? People often ask, "How much of RUP do we need to use to be able to say we run a RUP project?" Typically this question is relevant when a company requests a subcontractor to run a project according to RUP. It is also a relevant question during a step-by-step RUP implementation because people want to know how much RUP to implement before they can say they are finished.

In this chapter we give our view of what makes a project a RUP project. In what way is a RUP project "special"? In what way does it differ from a "normal" project? We begin with a description of some essential concepts in RUP followed by a definition of the spirit of RUP and the proposal that the members of a RUP project team should share their wisdom.

Finally, we list a few things to avoid when using RUP—the seven sins of a RUP project.

Those who are new to RUP might find some strange words and concepts in this chapter. We do not aim to give an exhaustive description of RUP in this book; instead, we refer you to other books that do [Kruchten 2000, Kroll and Kruchten 2003]. In this chapter we need to use some of the concepts in RUP in order to explain what characteristics make a RUP project special. If you are unfamiliar with these concepts, you may want to skip this chapter for now and read it later.

3.1   Essential Concepts in RUP

RUP will guide you in your effort to develop software. It contains information about practically all aspects of software development, such as how to plan your project, work with the vision and the business case, build prototypes, manage changes, and so on. These things you can find in other processes as well, but what makes RUP special is its completeness and configurability.

A RUP project should use RUP as a base for its process. When running the project, some parts of RUP might be excluded and others altered. If the project excludes a lot of the concepts in RUP, you might start to question whether the project really is a RUP project. If in doubt, bear in mind the basic principles of RUP (see "The Spirit of RUP" later in this chapter). Does your project follow those principles? The underlying intention of RUP can be described using the essential concepts described here. You could argue that other processes include one or more of these concepts as well, but RUP includes them all.

3.1.1   RUP Is Iterative

In the traditional method of planning projects, often called *waterfall development* [Royce 1998], the whole project is planned at once and the type of work performed is what distinguishes the phases. Basically, all requirements are defined in the beginning of the project. Designing the system and writing the code takes place somewhere in the middle, and all tests are performed at the end just before delivery. This way of organizing and planning software development typically leads to some problems, such as inability to act on changes in the requirements (there is only one entry and one planning session: the beginning of the project), late discovery of design errors (coding starts relatively late), quality issues due to lack of time for testing, and so on.

In modern management of software development projects, the iterative approach is followed. What do we mean by *iterative development?* Is it any different than *incremental development?* Let us consult RUP itself.

> Iteration: A distinct sequence of activities with a base-lined plan and valuation criteria resulting in a release (internal or external).

> Increment: The difference (*delta*) between two releases at the end of subsequent iterations.

Iterations and *increments* are often mixed up; people believe they have the same meaning. But if you think about how you can measure or express them, things might become clearer. An iteration can be measured in time, while an increment can be measured in the number of code lines, subsystems, or requirements implemented. An increment of the system is produced during an iteration. This means that the sequence of requirements, design, code, and test is repeated several times during a project (as shown in Figure 3.1), adding an increment of functionality to the product at every pass.

To be able to say that you work according to RUP, you need to plan and manage projects in an iterative fashion. Generally there will be more than one iteration in at least the Elaboration and Construction phases. However, a small, short project may have only one iteration per phase. At a glance,

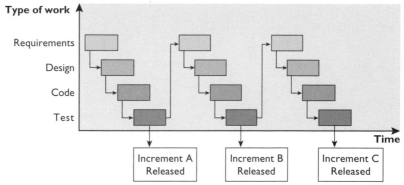

Figure 3.1   *Each iteration results in the release of an increment of the product. Experiences and results from an iteration affect the planning of the project as a whole and the content of the next iteration. Note that early releases are used internally and not delivered to the end user.*

such a project could look like a waterfall project with just different names for the development stages. But it is important to note that with RUP, each iteration (a phase in this case) results in a release. In some extreme cases when a project's duration is a few weeks or less, iterative development might not feel convenient because the iterations get too short. However, experience shows that even one-person projects can benefit from planning iterations (where the smallest possible number is three, one covering the Inception and Elaboration phases, one each for the Construction and Transition phases). The reason for this is that even for a small project it is important to take care of risks and validate an architecture early.

3.1.2   Planning in RUP Is Driven by Risks

RUP promotes risk reduction by advocating that a project should organize its work to systematically address and mitigate risks as early as possible in the project. Risks can be divided into several subgroupings (e.g., technical risks, economic risks, risks due to lack of competence, and so on). Risks need to be identified early in the project, along with their potential impacts and possible alternatives to eliminate or reduce them.

Creating (or even maintaining) a risk list, however, is not enough to be able to claim that the project follows RUP. The primary issue is how the knowledge of the risks influences the project planning, especially when deciding in what order to build the increments of the system. *Start with the part of the system that worries you the most, and you are probably on the right track.* Be careful, though: If you underestimate the consequences of a technical problem, you might not worry about it enough! It might go against your nature, but you should build the most risky part of the system first. This approach comes with two main benefits.

1. Your selected technical solution will be verified early in the project, reducing uncertainties. If the initial approach does not work, you will be able to evaluate alternatives before too much work has been invested. If the product proves to be impossible to build, you will be able to cancel the project before too much money is lost.
2. The predictability of the project's schedule and budget will improve as the project progresses.

To be able to say that you work according to RUP, you need to create and maintain a risk list, revisit the risks several times during the project (preferably at every project meeting, but at least after every iteration), and use the risk list as a tool and driver in the project planning. We see this as mandatory.

3.1.3 RUP Is Architecture Centric

Let's start by quoting RUP.

> Architecture: The highest level concept of a system in its environment, according to *IEEE* [The Institute of Electrical and Electronics Engineers]. The architecture of a software system (at a given point in time) is its organization or structure of significant *components* interacting through *interface*s, those components being composed of successively smaller components and interfaces.

The main focus of one of the phases in RUP, Elaboration, is to build the architecture of the system. By saying *build* we mean more than creating models showing subsystems, interfaces, and so on. These and other technical investigations do need to be performed, but what makes RUP a special process is that the architecture should be *executable*. Code should be written, tests should be performed. A paper-only architecture will not prove that your solution will work. You need to run and test the code to be sure.

To be able to say that you work according to RUP, architecture needs to play a central role in your project. Furthermore, the architecture should be verified by implementing (coding) and testing parts of the system before doing the bulk of the implementation.

3.1.4 RUP Is Driven by Use Cases

We stated earlier that risks should be used as the basis for planning the system. Another useful parameter to consider when planning is use cases. By defining functional requirements using the use case technique, the content of an iteration can be expressed in terms of which use cases (or parts thereof) should be implemented in the iteration. Saying that RUP is use case driven means that the creation of other models (e.g., the design model, the implementation model) as well as the test artifacts will "take off" from the use case model. Sometimes you will hear people say that RUP is *model driven*, meaning that there are defined ways to create a model from the information found in other models.

This approach will give you *traceability* between different descriptions of the system. One example of traceability is that you will be able to determine whether you have defined test cases for all intended ways to use the system. Use cases add several other benefits as well. One is that they steer you to focus first on how the user will benefit from the system, before you think about the technical solutions. Another example is that if stakeholders in the system and the development team have different views on how the system should be used, this will become painfully obvious during the modeling workshops. One person once said, "This method is great—we have never been angry at each other this early in a project before!" This may sound silly, but it is really much better to be angry at each other while defining the requirements than when the system has been deployed (Figure 3.2).

Figure 3.2   *It is better to have arguments when defining the requirements than after the delivery of the system.*

Even though we think use cases are great, we have seen situations where RUP has been used successfully without using use cases. Some organizations have well-established processes for requirements management and opt to continue using these techniques after introducing RUP. In this case a configuration of RUP will need to be created, showing how the requirement work connects to the rest of the process.

3.2   The Spirit of RUP

After reading this far you probably understand that working according to RUP is not about which document templates you use in your project. Yes, RUP will provide you with templates, advice, instructions, and tons of other useful stuff. But when it comes to answering the question "What is a RUP project?" we need to consider whether the project has been planned and executed according to the underlying principles, or "the spirit of RUP" of RUP [Kroll and Kruchten 2003]. But what is that spirit? When working with organizations, we use a checklist to evaluate whether their development projects adhere to RUP. The most important characteristics of the spirit of RUP are listed below.[1]

- Risks are handled early.
- The project stays focused on delivering value to the customer.
- The project is extremely focused on creating working software (code).
- Changes are accommodated throughout the project and as early as possible.
- An executable architecture is baselined early in the project.
- The system is built using components.
- All contributors to the product work closely together as a team.
- The project team is focused on quality during the whole project and does not have to worry about that in the end (at least no major surprises will surface at the end of the project).

Working according to these principles is actually more important than what roles, activities, and artifacts are used by the project. Following RUP will help you follow this spirit.

---

1. See Kroll and Kruchten [2003] for another description of the spirit of RUP.

3.3   RUP Project Team Members Share Their Wisdom

As you start to use RUP in your organization and your projects, you will make decisions about what parts of RUP to use, when to use them, how to use different tools, how to set up parameters, and so on. The rest of this book will be focused on these issues, but we want to emphasize here the importance of documenting these kinds of decisions.

When you think about it, what is it that makes RUP so valuable? For one thing, a lot of intelligent people with much experience have taken the time to document their views of how software should be developed. Why not continue that tradition? Almost every user of RUP will come up with a reusable way to apply RUP to a specific environment. Use the concept of guidelines! These kinds of simple documents describing smart things give a great return on investment (see Chapter 10, "Documenting Your Process").

3.4   The Seven Sins of a RUP Project

It is not easy to develop software. Even though you follow the principles behind RUP and consult RUP itself when planning and executing your projects, you can still fall into traps that may cause your project to fail. Below we discuss some of the most common traps, or sins, that can arise during a project—things that you want to avoid.[2]

- Planning to death
- Detailing too much
- Skipping problem analysis
- Letting end dates of iterations slip
- Starting the Construction phase before fulfilling the exit criteria of the Elaboration phase
- Testing only at the end of the project
- Failing to move the product to maintenance

---

2. Other authors such as Craig Larman, Philippe Kruchten, Kurt Bittner, and Barclay Brown have elaborated on similar topics in various papers.

3.4.1   Planning to Death

What are the responsibilities of a project manager? There are several, of course, but among the more crucial are finding the best people possible for the project and delivering the product in a timely and cost-effective manner. In order to do this, some milestones are defined so that the progress of the project can be measured. For a small project, this may be enough. The project manager can define delivery dates for the final product as well as the intermediate releases and measure the team's performance against those.

Larger projects require more planning to manage the resources in a more optimal way. There is also a need for other measurement points apart from the intermediate releases. A common mistake, however, is to try to plan activities on a too-detailed level too far in advance. Making overly detailed plans of who will do what six months from now is not useful. We do not even know exactly what part of the system will be under development at that point.

It might feel like you'll lose control over your project if you do not plan the whole project on a detailed level at once, and *this is in fact one of the major fears for a project manager leading a iterative project for the first time*. The problem with detailed plans, however, is that they need to be updated frequently or they will become outdated. The solution is to make a high-level plan and to complement this with a detailed plan per iteration, called *just-in-time planning*.

By *planning to death*, we mean that if a project manager tries to make a detailed plan for the whole project before starting the project, no development work will ever get done. The project team will feel too restrained by the plans, and all creativity will be lost. Furthermore, detailed plans that are created too early are almost always wrong because they are based on guesses and assumptions rather than real knowledge and up-to-date information.

Although iterative development adds complexity to the management of the project, it comes with advantages that will compensate for the extra effort. For example, *predictability* increases the further into the project you get. To quote a project manager who had completed his first iterative development project, "The main difference between managing traditional projects and iterative projects is that instead of having a bleeding ulcer the last few months of the project, you will have a healthy tension in your stomach during the whole project."

3.4.2   Detailing Too Much

This sin is common when a team that moves to iterative development normally has its roots in a waterfall way of thinking. For instance, the requirements should be defined and detailed only to a level that allows the project to move on to analysis and design for the current increment. After each iteration the work is evaluated; the situation as a whole is examined and the project scope, priorities, and so on might be altered. If all requirements are detailed to the lowest level too early, that work might be wasted.

3.4.3   Skipping Problem Analysis

Far too often, project teams start the work of defining requirements, choosing technology, and so on without considering what problem the system is supposed to solve! If the problem is not understood, it does not matter how good a system we build. No one wants a perfect system that solves the wrong problem. Actually, many projects fail because they deliver a good solution to the wrong problem. The system to be built needs to be connected to a business need, and this can be achieved only through a proper problem analysis.

3.4.4   Letting End Dates of Iterations Slip

We discussed earlier that the plan of the project should not be too detailed. What should be in the overall plan, however, are the target dates of the major milestones. In order to meet those dates, the project manager will define a number of iterations per phase and define goals for those. If the end date of an iteration slips, it is likely that the date for a major milestone will slip as well.

Our recommendation is that if it becomes impossible to meet the end date of an iteration, the scope of the iteration should be redefined (moving some parts to the next iteration) instead of letting the end date slip. Without getting into a detailed discussion of how to plan the content of the iterations, we want to point out that if this planning is done following the advice in RUP (prioritizing based on risk, architecture, and customer needs), all planned content of an iteration that recently ended will be more important than any of the content of the next iteration.

When moving functionality to be developed from one iteration to the next in order to keep the iteration's end date, we suggest two alternatives. One is to add resources in the next iteration to produce more work during the same time. The other is to move some chunks from the second iteration to the third. Just beware of the "snowplow effect" of pushing more and more of the system forward in time. Delays need to be taken care of sooner or later or the whole system will not be finished on the target release date. If it becomes impossible to catch up, an iteration needs to be added (letting the end date of the project slip) or the scope of the system being built needs to be reduced.

3.4.5 Starting Construction before Fulfilling the Exit Criteria of Elaboration

If there is one milestone in RUP that is more important than the others, it is the completion of the Elaboration phase (the lifecycle architecture milestone). Among other things, the architecture milestone specifies that it can be passed only if all of the following conditions are met.

*   The vision and the requirements are stable.
*   The architecture is stable.
*   The approach to be used during testing is proven.
*   An executable prototype demonstrates that all technical risks have been handled.

Furthermore, at this point of the project commitments are made to invest extensively by adding more resources to the project group.

If this milestone is passed without fulfilling the above-mentioned criteria, there is a risk that work will be spent on parts of the design that will need to be redone later because of changed technologies or sudden big changes in the requirements. Thus, the financial risk of the project will be much greater. It is also almost impossible to make good use of parallel development without a stable architecture. If parallel development is needed in order to meet the project schedule, extra emphasis should be given to this milestone.

Although most project teams are aware of the consequences, it is far too common to start the Construction phase before the exit criteria of the Elaboration phase are met to "save time." Don't do that.

3.4.6   Testing Only at the End of the Project

RUP tells us that testing of the product should be done in each iteration. The advantages of this are that the debugging of the system will start early, any performance issues will be found while there is still time to correct them, and there will not be a bulk of testing to do at the end of the project. However, testing tends to be something "special" or "separate" in some organizations, making it hard to integrate with the rest of the development disciplines in a good way (often due to issues of organizational culture). Because of this, it becomes "easy" to exclude testing from the iterative work by using a mix of iterative and waterfall development where everything but testing is performed iteratively, leaving testing until the end of the project just as in waterfall development. By doing this, however, we lose the test-related advantages of iterative development and also risk that issues within the requirements and design will not be revealed until the end of the project.

Furthermore, if test professionals are involved during the whole project, deficiencies regarding security, recovery procedures, and so on can be revealed earlier.

3.4.7   Failing to Move the Product to Maintenance

This problem is not really specific to RUP, but it might be more common to fall into this trap when starting to work iteratively. If maintenance is seen as just another iteration on the product, the project group that developed the product will still be responsible for the product. But most likely the members of the project group have moved on to new challenges and maintenance of the "old" product will not be a priority. It is better to move the responsibility for the product from the project group to a function within the organization that can monitor the need for maintenance, make small fixes, and start a new project if more extensive maintenance work is needed.

3.5   Conclusion

One RUP project can differ a lot from another RUP project. The important thing is to follow the spirit of RUP when choosing which parts of it to use in a project. All RUP projects use risks as a basis for planning and build the architecture early in the project. Most develop software iteratively using use cases to define the functional requirements. Team members who have used RUP for a while apply more of the essential concepts in RUP, such as accommodating changes as soon as possible and staying focused on the system to be delivered. They will also know that a good problem analysis is the key to a successful project.

In the next chapter, we will look at the first major step of a RUP adoption: how to assess the current situation.

4

Assessing Your Organization

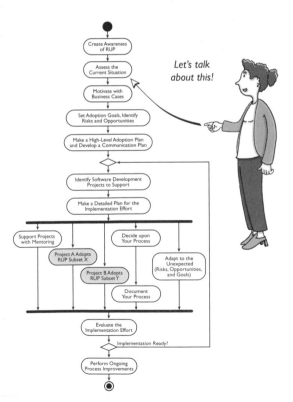

Let's talk about this!

Imagine hiking in the woods. You have a map and a compass. On the map there is an X marking your destination, and before you left several hours ago, someone said you should move northeast to reach your goal. There's only one problem: You found some nice berries while making your way through the woods. You like berries, so you tasted some, saw some more, ate some more . . . now you are lost! Will you get to your goal? No, not unless you can figure out where you are on the map and use your compass to find out what direction to move in (Figure 4.1).

When you're introducing a new way to work in an organization, you're in a similar situation. There will most likely be a goal, an idea of how the organization should function after the change of process. But before you can figure

Figure 4.1   *Make sure to find out where you are before starting to move!*

out what steps to take in order to get to the desired situation, the current state of your organization needs to be determined. In RUP this is called *assessing the current organization*. The word *assessment* might seem very formal, but in short it is all about finding out how an organization works with software development today, what *pains* it experiences, and in what ways it needs to improve.

There are several things to evaluate. This chapter walks you through what to do. First we discuss the importance of finding out why the assessment is being made and who wants it. After that we describe how to begin the assessment. Later more detailed sections cover how to perform the actual assessment and what to look for. Finally we round out this chapter by giving some advice on how to compile your findings into a report and a presentation.

4.1   Who Wants the Assessment and Why?

Before the assessment starts, it is wise to get some clarification. Who is interested in the result of the assessment? How do people feel about it?

Assessments are typically needed only when an organization is considering a change. The reasons for the change might vary, as well as how the assessment is initiated. Some of the most common situations are listed below.

- You suspect that your organization needs to improve but you have no clear understanding of how.
- Your organization needs an outside view of the situation in order to motivate changes you already know are needed.
- Someone has sold the assessment to your organization and people found it a rational thing to do.

To successfully assess an organization, you need to accomplish two things first.

- Identify the persons who will be affected by the assessment and the changes that might result from it.
- Understand the underlying reasons for starting the change and who is initiating it.

You will need to set the expectations right. The organization's processes will not change solely by making an assessment, nor is it possible to find *all* the right recommendations. An assessment is the first important step in the change process within the organization, not the final step.

4.2   Kicking Off the Assessment

When attempting to make changes of any kind in an organization, providing information to the people who will be affected by the change is essential. If people are not informed, they might get worried and meet the change with resistance, which complicates the change effort.

Because the assessment is the first step in the change process, its purpose, content, and procedure need to be carefully communicated. This is best done in a *kickoff meeting* attended by all the people who will be involved or affected by the process changes. As many managers of affected staff as possible need to be present because their support is essential to the success of the process implementation. The change starts with the kickoff meeting! A process will start in people's brains; this process will be described in more detail in Chapter 5, "Motivating the RUP Adoption," and Chapter 11, "A Guide to Successful Mentoring."

The assessment kickoff meeting starts with a basic overview of RUP and its best practices. The purpose of this is to create a common understanding of the process and its role for different aspects of development. The presentation should also emphasize that RUP is nothing magic. It is mostly common sense, packaged in a wise way. Some expressions and concepts need to be introduced to begin familiarizing the team with a new common language to use when talking about software development.

Apart from presenting RUP and how RUP can help an organization, the kickoff meeting should also focus on how the assessment will be performed. Before the meeting you need to tell organizational representatives which people and roles need to be interviewed during the assessment. During the meeting you should focus on explaining the purpose of the interviews and what types of questions will be asked. Take the opportunity to ask for current process material and project documentation from recently completed projects. The *assessors* will be exposed to confidential information, and if they are external to the organization, they will likely need to sign nondisclosure agreements before reading documentation and starting the interviews. When consultants perform the assessment, the nondisclosure agreement should cover the entire consultant company in order to enable discussions of findings and conclusions with colleagues.

Set the expectations for the assessment during the meeting. The assessment will not cure any problems in the organization. Explain that the assessment will identify areas of improvement and suggest actions to achieve better productivity. A lot of work will have to be done after the assessment, but the assessment will be the essential activity that identifies this work. To put it another way, the assessment will not result in a detailed adoption plan but will describe possible steps in the plan and their order.

Make clear to the people present at the kickoff meeting that the answers from the upcoming interviews will be treated with confidence. No names will be mentioned in the assessment report, and measures will be taken to make sure criticism cannot be traced to individuals. People tend to be more open about the situation during the interviews if they realize this.

4.3   How to Assess

How is the information found? There are, of course, many methods for finding information (many are described in RUP itself). In the assessment situation, the four most beneficial methods are those listed below.

1. Interview people in the organization.
2. Read existing process material, project documentation, and so on.
3. Compare the organization with others, based on the assessors' knowledge.
4. Observe people during actual work. In some cases people perform work in ways other than what they describe during interviews or in written descriptions. However, this method is more time consuming than the other three.

Experiences show that a team of at least two to three assessors makes the assessment more beneficial. When deriving conclusions and making recommendations, different people's views of the situation are useful. Within a team, ideas can be discussed and analyzed, which is crucial to ensure that the situation has been correctly interpreted.

4.3.1   Interviewing People

Interviews are an effective technique for assessment because people in your organization are the number one source of information. After all, they're the ones who perform the work and know how it's done. What a process description says is of less importance. As the RUP says, "A process description is not a process"; the process is the way work actually is performed.

During the kickoff meeting (if not earlier) a list of people to interview is created. Normally 15–20 people need to be interviewed in a mid-sized organization (50–200 developers) to get enough information about the situation. If the number of interviewees is too small, there is a risk that all those people belong to the same unofficial group within the organization; possible communication problems with other groups may be missed.

Should one person be interviewed at a time or can several people be present? Interviewing two people at a time has many benefits. Obviously it saves time because fewer interviews are required. The interaction between the two people creates a more open atmosphere during the interview. The assessors can obtain more than one view of a specific topic at the same time, and some related information may emerge after one person hears the other talk. If you decide to interview two people at once, what "pairs" are better than others? Try to pair up people who normally don't talk to each other enough. For example, interview a project manager and a customer representative together, and pair a business analyst with a developer. In some cases, however, pairing up project managers from two different kinds of projects can prove to be very productive.

A good habit is to reconnect to statements from previous interviews when interviewing. This gives the assessor a good picture of the communication in the organization and illustrates whether there is a common understanding of the current process. Techniques for interviewing are not covered in any great depth in this book (additional information can be found in RUP), but here are the most important aspects to remember.

- Use a list of prepared questions to make sure you don't forget any areas. (The tables that appear later in this chapter present some examples.)
- Ask open, context-free questions, and encourage spontaneous reflections by the interviewees.
- Do not bias the interview with your understanding of the organization so far; instead, try to get *another* view of situations on which you already have some information.

In addition to interviewing two people at a time, you can consider having two people conduct the interview. To prevent a loss of focus, one person should ask the majority of the questions while the other person takes notes, preferably using a laptop.[1] Having the notes in an electronic format saves time when writing the report. The second person can also ask follow-up questions when appropriate. (Sometimes the main interviewer, who is focused on getting answers to the prepared questions, might miss important "hints" in interviewee responses that should be pursued further. The second interviewer can more easily watch for such opportunities.)

4.3.2   Reading Process Documentation

Although what people say during the interviews is more important than what a process description says, some time should be spent reading the current process documentation. There are cases where the description on paper is really good, but people in the organization do not follow it. If this situation occurs, it is very important to find out why people don't use the current documented process and to identify actions to remove the reasons. You do not want to introduce just another process that will not be used! Try to find out whether the presentation of the process description fits the organization. Culture and habits affect the best way to communicate the process to individuals.

4.3.3   Comparing with Other Organizations

If the team performing the assessment has experiences with other similar organizations, comparisons should be done. The material and knowledge gained from performing assessments is highly confidential, but it is often possible to consolidate good practices that make organizations successful *without* mentioning confidential information.

4.4   What to Assess

During the assessment the assessors will look for information about the organization and its practices in order to find improvement areas. What types of information should they look for? Roughly, the information can be divided into the following categories:

---

1. Another method is to use a tape recorder to complement handwritten notes; this enables the assessment team to go back to the tape when discussing conclusions.

- People
- Organization
- Types of products and projects
- Supporting tools
- The current process
- The description of the current process

These categories are discussed below. Each subsection contains a table that shows what areas need to be covered at a minimum. These questions are not an exhaustive list, but simply examples to give you an idea of what questions need to be asked.

4.4.1   People

What *groupings* of people occur in your organization? Groups may be divided by technical competence (e.g., Cobol and Java), by attitudes toward change, or just by different personalities. Different types of individuals or groups of individuals relate differently to change. In order to suggest the best strategies for implementing the process, the current conditions need to be known.

Identify the *informal leaders*. These people have the attention of the masses, and their opinions affect lots of other people. Normally it is good to involve these informal leaders in the group (project team) that will guide and manage the change later.

Some organizations depend on *external consultants*. If this is the case in your situation, it is important to clarify what roles the external consultants have. If the consultants have competence in using another process that differs from the one to be introduced, they may resist the change because their assignments may appear to be in danger. Another risk is that the implementation will be endangered when one or more consultants leave the organization for other assignments. Of course, this risk is valid for regular employees as well, but consultants tend to move between assignments more often than people change jobs. We have even seen cases where consultants benefited from an implementation by getting free education on RUP and then left the organization!

Table 4.1 indicates the areas to cover when assessing people.

Area to Be Covered	Helps Determine	Examples of Questions to Ask
How much "pain" the people in the organization feel	Their motivation to change. A successful change requires strongly motivated people. People who think things are already fine tend to be less motivated to change.	• Are there areas within development work that cause you problems today? • Have you had experiences when the documents or other material on which you base your work were faulty or incomplete? • Do you feel that the development in this organization is controlled and predictable?
Knowledge of RUP and other processes	The need for training and communication.	• How much do you know about RUP? • Are you used to following a defined process? If so, which? • Have you taken part in iterative development?
Attitudes toward RUP and toward change in general	The need for communication and visible management support.	• Do you feel there is a need to change the process in this organization? • Has the purpose for the change been communicated? • Do you think RUP is the right process to implement?

Table 4.1   *Areas to Cover When Assessing People*

4.4.2   The Organization

How is the organization structured? Is it in one place or scattered all over the world? Is it hierarchical? Divided into business units[2] or by functions?[3] These questions are fairly easy to answer just by looking at an *organization chart*. But the boxes in an organization chart are one thing; how work actually is performed, that's another! The unofficial organization needs to be found.

What are the relationships between different departments? Between management and the project teams? How is the communication? Normally the communication in an organization is good. Deficiencies are usually

---

2. A business unit is typically responsible for a product or a system and is self-supporting in competence (i.e., its people have skills in many disciplines).
3. In a function organization, or a matrix organization, employees are grouped according to their skills, (e.g., all analysts make up one team, all developers another, and so on) and are "loaned" to projects.

caused by lack of *structured communication.* The informal channels of communication are fast and efficient; however, it is easy to forget to include some receivers, which is especially bad when the information is important. In some organizations the relationship between two departments might even be hostile. If that is the case, the reason behind the hostility needs to be investigated. The cause may be a history of mergers, bad experiences in recent projects, or just the lack of a common language, which makes it hard for the departments to communicate with each other.

The things mentioned here, among others, indicate the organization's *capacity for change,* that is, how much change the organization can endure during a specific period of time. Although each organization is different, if the assessors do not have enough past experiences or examples to compare with, they might not be able to determine the capacity for change. In these cases a good practice is to take a small first step, evaluate, and then replan the whole implementation if necessary. Some more general indicators of the capacity for change can be found if the organization has gone through other changes recently. If it has been successful with those changes, it is more likely that the organization will be successful in adopting RUP as well.

Table 4.2 indicates the areas to cover when assessing the organization.

4.4.3   Types of Products and Projects

As discussed elsewhere in the book, each organization needs to tailor RUP to make it specific to the organization's situation. The types of projects an organization runs affects the dividing of the development cycle into phases and milestones. Two common situations are speculative development and acquirer–supplier development.

In speculative development you don't know your end customer when you start the project. The idea is to develop something and sell it when it is finished (much like the way common desktop applications are developed). A project group in this situation needs to have very strict reviews of the business case and initial requirements. Reference groups will be involved, and most likely the exit criteria of some milestones will need to be refined.

In *acquirer–supplier development* you already know your customer. However, a customer who orders the development of a product often requests

Area to Be Covered	Helps Determine	Examples of Questions to Ask
The number of "units" in the organization and their physical distribution	How to structure the implementation regarding the number of pilot projects and so on	• Can you describe what units/departments in the organization get involved in software development? • Does a project normally involve people from different locations? • Are different types of development (domains, types of projects, and so on) handled in different parts of the organization?
The different communication channels that exist (official and unofficial)	How to develop a communication plan for the change effort	• What happens when a customer suggests a change to a system being developed? How does the developer get to know about the change? • How does the project team communicate with other departments (marketing, sales, operation, and so on)?
The ability to change	How much of RUP can be adapted in each step	• What major changes have taken place in this organization before, and how did these make you feel? • Have you been affected by a process implementation before in your career? What were your experiences? • Do you feel this organization is adaptable and friendly to changes?

Table 4.2   *Areas to Cover When Assessing the Organization*

a "fixed price" for the project at an early stage. Estimation of iterative projects is not within the scope of this book, but the fixed-price issue can be summarized briefly this way: "Your cost estimate will get better and better the further into the project you go." At some point, however, you will need to give a price. It is preferable to wait until the end of the Elaboration phase, but if that is not possible, a new milestone in the middle of Elaboration could be introduced to ensure that the price will be based on the best possible metrics.

When it comes to *technical complexity,* the axis spans from stand-alone, client-based applications to advanced integrated systems with high-performance requirements. In short, the more technically complex a system you are building, the more you need a formal process.

Area to Be Covered	Helps Determine	Examples of Questions to Ask
Typical types of projects run in the organization	Suitable lifecycle models (one or more)	• How is a project financed? • If fixed prices are used, when is the price set? • How are the initial requirements defined?
The complexity of the development (technical and managerial)	The appropriate formality for the future process (e.g., how to work with reviews)	• What is the relationship between functional and nonfunctional requirements when it comes to the complexity of implementation? • How many people are usually on a project team? • Are hierarchical project structures used? With what number of subprojects?
Drivers in development	What the process *must* ensure; the trade-off between agility and formality	• What is most important—a low development cost, a quick time to market, completion of the functional requirements, or high quality? • Is it acceptable to your customers to have functionality delivered in additional packages after the initial delivery? • Do you need to adhere to legal requirements regarding quality and reviews?

Table 4.3   *Areas to Cover When Assessing Types of Products and Projects*

Another product-related aspect to cover is what is most important for the final result. Is it quality, reliability, or maybe cost per user? The answer will tell you what parts of the process to implement, how formally to work with reviews, and so on.

How big are typical projects in terms of the *number of project members?* How long do they take to complete? Does the organization work with teams of teams? Answers to these types of questions help you choose a subset of RUP and also determine how quickly the total implementation can be done.

Table 4.3 indicates the areas to cover when assessing products and projects.

4.4.4   Supporting Tools

Tool support needs to be considered when implementing RUP. Some time-consuming activities are most likely automated already in the cur-

Area to Be Covered	Helps Determine	Examples of Questions to Ask
The current level of tool support	Possible tools to integrate	• What tools are used today and for what purposes? What are your experiences from using these tools? • Are there areas where you see a need for tool support? • Have you experienced problems due to lack of tool integration?

Table 4.4   *Areas to Cover When Assessing Tools*

rent process. The individuals will not be motivated to adapt to a new process that adds manual work to the areas that previously were automated. It may be possible to keep some of the existing tools in the new environment; some may have to be replaced because they will not function in the new process; and some new areas may need to be addressed. The types of questions that need to be asked include the following: What tools are used today? Will they support an iterative process when the organization is ready to introduce it? What part of the current process do the tools help the employees with? Are there areas that currently lack tool support? Has that led to any problems?

Table 4.4 indicates the areas to cover when assessing tools.

4.4.5   The Current Process

All organizations have a process. It just may not be documented. There may even be more than one! However, if there is a process, people will compare the new process with the existing one. Most likely some parts of the current process work perfectly, and those parts that can be integrated with the new process should be retained, at least at first. It is important to figure out which areas are perceived as cumbersome in today's process, which areas lack a common process, and whether there are areas where work is done in different ways depending on individuals, departments, projects, and so on.

People in the organization need to be able to relate to the old process: "Oh yes, now we are going to create a software architecture document. That contains almost the same information as our old implementation proposals." To succeed in helping people through this change, the RUP mentors need to have knowledge about the old process as well as the new one based on RUP.

Some common process-related problems can indicate the feasibility of improvements in the current process. Let's look at some examples.

- **Problem 1: Scope Creep**
  The requirements collection process performed early in the project might be good. Budgeting and scheduling are done according to accepted rules. But the projects tend to overrun budgets and time estimates. Why? One reason may be that functionality is added to the product as development progresses. This often indicates that the management part of requirements management has been forgotten. As change requests appear, the scope of the project needs to be reconsidered and budget and schedules updated. This is one of the key aspects of iterative development: Update the plans as needed when you change something in the project. Remember, though, that iterative development needs to be planned for—it doesn't just happen because of badly managed requirements and scope creep.

- **Problem 2: Inability to Capture Requirements**
  This is the most common area for possible improvements in organizations. Requirements management is often the first part of RUP to implement. If all requirements are not found, or if the requirements found are not fully understood, the result will be a system that will not meet the expectations of the stakeholders. What are the reasons for poor requirements capture? The three main reasons are listed below.

  - The background was not explored, so the development team does not know why the system should be built (the problem it is supposed to solve) and thus does not know what questions to ask.
  - Not all of the stakeholders were found, so the development team does not ask the right people for requirements.
  - The requirements were misunderstood due to ambiguous descriptions and communication.

- **Problem 3: Inability to Manage Requirements**
  This problem is related to scope creep. It may be that the number of requirements has not changed, but some of the requirements *themselves* may have changed without the project team knowing about it or

being able to realize how it affects the system. The result is that the product delivered does not satisfy the needs of the stakeholders.

- **Problem 4: Poor Schedule Estimation**
  Scheduling (together with cost estimates) is one of the most discussed areas within software development. It is rather easy to detect whether an organization's projects are finished according to plan or not. If delays are common, the first challenge you face is to find out why. Scope creep and poor requirements management may be the cause, but the estimation itself can also be the problem. Are estimates based on guesses? If historical data is used, it might not be relevant to the organization's current projects.

- **Problem 5: Design Deficiencies**
  Does the organization have a history of rebuilding systems rather than extending them? Does it get harder and harder to implement changes in existing systems? Do changes tend to destabilize builds? Do changes to one component tend to break other components? These things often indicate a problem with defining an architecture. There might be a clearly defined way to solve technical aspects of a system, but these guidelines might not be communicated in a good way, or there might be other reasons why people do not follow them.

- **Problem 6: Poor-Quality Products**
  This problem is usually caused by insufficient time to test (which in turn often is a symptom of other problems, such as failure to manage requirements and changes, inadequate staffing, and so on). Another reason for quality problems may be that the test specifications are not connected to the requirements, resulting in incorrect system testing or no testing at all for parts of the system. One aspect regarding quality and iterative development is that some organizations fail to implement iterative testing. Tests are performed according to RUP but are placed at the end of the project schedule. This does not necessarily mean that the product quality will be low, but rather that many of the benefits from the iterative development will be lost. When tests are part of an iteration, the project team has a chance to take corrective actions *before* the product reaches the end customer.

- **Problem 7: Out-of-Sync Product and Documentation**
  We sometimes encounter a customer who wants to have "some new functionality" implemented in an existing system. The development

team retrieves the documentation from the archives, looks at the requirements and the design model, and makes the needed changes to the design. To finalize the job the team goes into the code and realizes that the code does not correspond to the documentation. What happened? Probably the project team developing the product in the first place had to make some last-minute changes to accommodate customer needs and to correct defects, and there was no time to update the documentation before the deadline. After delivering the system, the team was dissolved and individuals left for new challenges. Maintenance of a system gets more difficult when there is a mismatch between the documentation and the product. Using a process that ensures that design and code stay in sync can solve some of these problems.

Table 4.5 indicates the areas to cover when assessing the current process.

Area to Be Covered	Helps Determine	Examples of Questions to Ask
Experiences of the current process	What parts of the current process to reuse and integrate with the new process	• Is there a process today? If yes, what parts are good, and what needs improvement? • Is the current process widely used? If not, why not?
Indicators of process-related problems	What areas most need process improvement	• Have you experienced the addition of new requirements late in the project? • Do you know which people will use or in other ways be affected by the system to be built? • In the past, has the project team ever misunderstood the requirements, or has the meaning of requirements changed during some projects? • How does your organization create size estimates for a project? • Is it easy to accommodate changes in parts of the system that have already been built? • How extensive is testing, and what are the typical results/feedback from testing? • What is the status of the design documentation at the end of the project? Is it sufficient as a basis for maintenance?

Table 4.5   *Areas to Cover When Assessing the Current Process*

4.4.6   The Current Process Description

How is the current process described? Are there detailed descriptions of activities or just checklists or document templates? Our experience shows that people often find it hard to quickly change from a documentation based only on checklists and templates to a more thorough documentation such as the activity descriptions in RUP. Are there areas that the current process description does not cover completely? Most likely this is the case; perhaps the undocumented process should be described as a first step of formalization.

Often there are areas in the current process description that are well described and potentially able to help the organization in its work. But the people in the organization don't follow the description! In that case, *it is important to figure out why.* There might be an unwillingness to use process descriptions as such, an issue with how the process has been presented, or maybe some political issue ("I'm certainly not going to do as they say!"). This needs to be investigated because the organization will not benefit much from a new process description that will not be used either. The important issue for the receiving organization is the process, not the process description; hence the description should be appealing and easy to put into practice. The description should help people follow the process, guiding them and providing information. Read more on this topic in Chapter 10, "Documenting Your Process."

Table 4.6 indicates the areas to cover when assessing the current process description.

Area to Be Covered	Helps Determine	Examples of Questions to Ask
The type of documentation currently used	The acceptable level of documentation for the new process	• How is the current process described? • Do you find certain parts of the documentation more useful than others? • Is it easy to find the information you need in the current process documentation? • For the parts of the process that currently lack documentation, what documentation would help you do your job?

Table 4.6   *Areas to Cover When Assessing the Current Process Description*

4.5   Compiling the Material

The assessors are back at the office with lots of transcripts from the interviews. Where should you begin, what should you look for? First, the transcripts should be put away and the spontaneous feelings from the previous days should be written down. After that, the transcripts should be searched for comments that support or contradict those feelings. Then a more formal read-through of the transcripts should take place. Discussions within the assessor team and, if possible, with colleagues who did not participate in the assessment effort are a vital part of the compilation work.

4.5.1   Identifying Problems

The aim should be to identify all the problems in the organization and to assign a "severity" rating to them. What impacts do the problems have on your organization's ability to develop high-quality software with high productivity? Most problems will not be acknowledged by everyone in the organization. Often the most serious problems suffered by some parts of the organization will not be perceived as a problem by other parts. For example, a customer representative sees acceptance of late changes in the requirements specification as good service to the customer, although it creates huge problems for a developer.

4.5.2   Drawing Conclusions

Problems found might be linked to each other, and some problems might not be problems at all but symptoms caused by other problems. So what are the root causes of the problems? Why do these problems occur like this in the organization? Should all problems be addressed? Is it possible to correct all problems? Sometimes external factors, out of the organization's control, cause a problem; then we need a way to *handle* the problem more than a way to *solve* it.

4.5.3   Formulating Recommendations

The recommendations should consist of what actions to take, in which order, and also in approximately how many steps to take them. Depending on the situation the recommendations could include revisiting conclusions and recommendations after a period of time.

4.6   The Assessment Report

A lot of quality time is spent on performing the assessment. All that effort should not be hidden behind a lot of words. Within RUP, a document template is provided to help you structure the report. People want to have easy access to the conclusions, so the report should not be too long; between 15 and 20 pages is normally sufficient. It is easy to fall into the trap of mentioning just the problems, but good things in the organization should also be documented. Some people may not know about the things that already work well. Besides, it makes reading the report much more enjoyable.

Remember that names should not be mentioned in the report! Failing to maintain the confidentiality of the information provided during interviews can destroy the trust that will be essential if the assessment leads to a process implementation.

The different stakeholders of the report need to be considered. *Top managers want to have a short summary of the situation and some clear recommendations.* The persons responsible for the implementation want to have more in-depth descriptions of the actions to take, the reasons behind them, and an idea of how difficult it will be to perform the activities. Time permitting; consider the preparation of more than one report—one for management, one for the process engineer, and one for the development teams. This makes it possible to point out the information that is of most importance to each group. Often it is enough to create just one report as long as there is a good summary of it.

UML was developed to improve communication among people involved in software development. An added benefit of UML is that you can use activity diagrams to present the recommendations from an assessment, showing in which order you recommend the activities be performed, which of them can be done in parallel, and so on. Figure 4.2 provides an example of a portion of such a diagram. Figure 4.3 shows the outline of an assessment report template recommended by RUP.

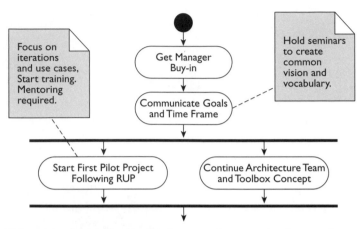

Figure 4.2   *Using a UML activity diagram to describe the steps of a process implementation*

---

1. *Introduction*
   1.1 *Purpose*
   1.2 *Scope*
   1.3 *Definitions, Acronyms, and Abbreviations*
   1.4 *References*
   1.5 *Overview*
2. *Business Context*
3. *External Factors*
   3.1 *Customers*
   3.2 *Competitors*
   3.3 *Other Stakeholders*
4. *Internal Factors*
   4.1 *Development Process*
   4.2 *Supporting Tools*
   4.3 *Internal Organization*
   4.4 *Competences, Skills, and Attitudes*
   4.5 *Capacity for Change*
5. *Product Characteristics*
   5.1 *Size of Software-Development Effort*
   5.2 *Degree of Novelty*
   5.3 *Type of Application*
   5.4 *Technical Complexity*
6. *Assessment Conclusions*
7. *Recommendations*

Figure 4.3   *Outline of the template for an assessment report (From RUP; reprinted with permission of IBM Rational.)*

4.7   Presentation of the Findings

The same audience that attended the kickoff meeting should also attend the presentation of the findings. People can read the report, so there is no need to present everything in detail. Focus on the key areas, their impacts, and the activities to perform. One possibility is to use a template organized around the best practices of RUP showing the strengths as well as possible improvements for each of the best practices. The main part is the recommendations. The presentation itself typically lasts around 20 minutes and ends with a slide showing the steps to take in order to improve the overall situation. However, it is not uncommon for the discussion that follows the presentation to take over an hour—the conclusions might be questioned! So the assessors need to prepare well.

Try to have senior management of the development organization in the room while presenting. This is the starting point for the next step in the implementation. Your organization (and management) need some time to digest the conclusions and recommendations before creating an implementation plan. Be available for discussions during this time.

Note that it might be necessary to have meetings with some of the interviewees in order to validate your conclusions before the main presentation. This is especially important if the assessment is very negative.

4.8   Conclusion

If you do not know how the work is done today, it is impossible to make a plan that leads to a new way of working. Also, it is a good practice to improve the weakest areas first. Therefore, these must be found. An assessment is performed by following these simple steps.

1. Find out who wants the assessment and why.
2. Kick off the assessment.
3. Decide how to make the assessment.
4. Decide what questions to ask and what to look for.
5. Compile your findings and draw conclusions.
6. Produce a report.
7. Present your findings.

In the next chapter, we will discuss the need to motivate the adoption both from a business perspective and for the people who will change their ways of working.

5

Motivating the RUP Adoption

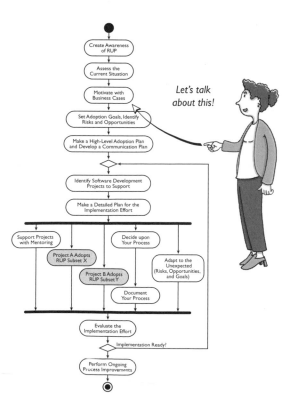

Let's talk
about this!

Before your organization decides to use RUP for all software development throughout the organization, it should be very clear *why*.

Introducing *change* to one or more processes in an organization is an investment. Most organizations do this because they want to benefit from the change, for example, to use more efficient processes or create higher quality products. Making an investment requires spending money at one point in time to create the possibility of a future profit.

Adopting RUP in an organization needs to be looked on as an *investment as well*. The initial expenses of money, time, and maybe some frustration lead to the profits of increased productivity, better quality, and more efficient teamwork.

A good investment gives a profit. A good adoption of RUP gives a higher value back than the value of the initial investment.

Creating a *business case* when defining why RUP shall be adopted within your organization forces you to think through what results you want to achieve and how to assign them monetary value. The business case will motivate the decision to adopt RUP in economic terms, but what about people? People will ask themselves and each other: "Why do we have to change? Is it really necessary?" and "Our way of working isn't that bad, is it?" These questions need to be answered; the adoption of *RUP needs to be motivated*.

This chapter discusses the benefits RUP can give an organization. We describe what to think about when creating a business case and how to use measurements to follow up after the adoption. We also discuss what effects the change to RUP may have on productivity and how people in the organization might feel and behave.

5.1   Motivating the Decision to Adopt RUP

To create a business case to define the business benefits of adopting RUP, we need to make assumptions about how much time we need to spend to adopt RUP and compare those assumptions with estimates of how much we will save when RUP is adopted. Although there are many possible reasons to adopt RUP, most of them are drilled down from a top-level goal to increase the profit of the organization; hence, productivity or cost savings are relevant for a business case. RUP adoption requires some initial costs in terms of licenses, training, and perhaps mentoring. The highest costs in the software industry, however, are salaries, and the time that people spend in the classroom attending training can often "cost" more than the course itself. Therefore, the most important aspect to consider in a business case is *people's productivity*.

Another aspect that affects the profit within our industry is quality. If the quality of a product is too low, it will not pass the final tests; rework will have to be done or, even worse, customer satisfaction will go down. However, let us leave the quality aspect for now and focus on productivity.

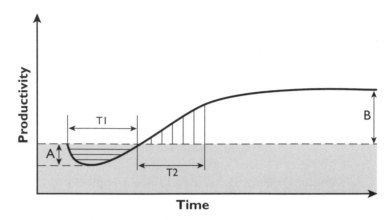

Figure 5.1   *When organizations introduce change, productivity decreases (A) before the benefits of the change can be noticed (B).*

When an organization introduces change of any kind, people tend to become less productive for a while before learning the new way of working, regaining the previous level of productivity, and finally reaching a new, hopefully higher productivity level (see Figure 5.1).

The smaller the *dip in productivity*, the better the business case, (A), and the greater the *increase in productivity* (B) that can be achieved from the change. Time is also of interest. The less time the productivity dip lasts, the better. After T1 weeks, productivity rises back to the level experienced before the change was introduced. The area in Figure 5.1 marked with horizontal lines *represents the investment* made by introducing the change (i.e., the investment caused by reduced productivity only, which tends to be higher than any investments in licenses, training, and so on). When the area marked with vertical lines becomes equal with the previous area, the *break-even point* has been reached. This means that after an additional T2 weeks following the first T1 weeks, you will start to gain from your investment in a new process.

5.1.1   Reducing the Productivity Dip

The smaller the productivity dip (A) and the shorter the amount of time it lasts (T1), the better the business case. How can we reduce A and T1? Do we always have to experience a productivity dip when adopting RUP?

Many of the suggestions in this book can help you reduce the dip.

- Adopt RUP in small steps.
- Decide upon and document your process as you go.
- Integrate RUP with existing processes.
- Use pilot projects.
- Communicate frequently.
- Use appropriate training.
- Use mentors to support the adoption.

The size of the dip also depends on the level of productivity before the process change. Ironically, an organization with a low productivity level may well experience a greater increase in productivity (B) than an organization that is already on a high productivity level. The reason is that for an organization with low productivity, changing only a minor part of the process has big effects, whereas it's harder to make improvements within an organization that already has fairly high productivity. Let's make a comparison from the world of sports. A beginner at golf will be able to improve his or her personal record significantly (e.g., by hitting the ball at all) by correcting only one basic fault in the technique used. For a golf champion to improve, many small things in the current technique need to be changed. During a period of time the results of the golf champion will be poorer than normal, but in the end hopefully better than before. Experiences show that by changing only a small part of the current process, the dip (A) will be small. By changing many parts of the current process at once, the dip will be big. The smaller A and the bigger B we can achieve, the better the business case!

In some cases, especially when an organization has big deficiencies in the area of problem analysis and requirements management, there might be *no noticeable dip* in productivity at all. By improving these critical areas, the organization might experience the payoff during the first project because the new process addresses previously serious problems in the old process (see Figure 5.2). The first project may well deliver under budget!

5.1.2   Increasing the Improvement

The greater the improvement in productivity (B) and the longer time we can benefit from it, the better the business case. But just what affects the productivity of a software development organization? COCOMO II, a

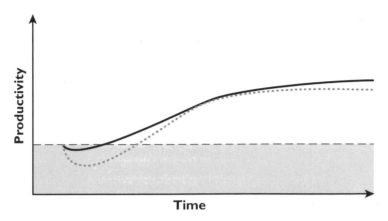

Figure 5.2   *In some cases the productivity dip will be very small or not noticed at all.*

model for estimating costs for software development, defines over twenty-five parameters that affect productivity [Boehm et al. 2000]. Among these, five strongly depend on the process used. Table 5.1 describes these five parameters together with rough figures of what to expect when improving them.

5.1.3   Comparing the Initial Investment and the Dip with the Improvement

Bringing it all together, an organization pays for the adoption of RUP by spending money on licenses for the process and tools, training expenses, and an initial decrease in productivity. The organization will eventually gain an increased productivity in the long run. A simplified example shows how a business case may look.

> A company with 50 developers has relatively small projects, which usually require 10 people to work full-time for 6 months. The organization's internal cost for a project member is $100/hour, giving an average project budget of 170 hours/month × 10 people × 6 months × $100/hour = $1,020,000.

> The initial investment covering tool licenses, training, and so on for the pilot project is $30,000. The pilot project experiences a 20% dip in productivity, which creates an extra cost for the project of .20 × $1,020,000 = $204,000. (Note that this cost is higher than the cost for licenses and training.) The total investment for the pilot project is $30,000 + $204,000 = $234,000.

Parameter	How Using RUP May Improve the Parameter	What to Expect after Improving It
Management of complexity	The introduction of a model-based notation (UML) makes it easier to understand the whole system and how it is built up by subsystems. It also becomes easier to communicate. New concepts for change and configuration management allow changes to be introduced in a controlled way in complex systems. New methods for scope management make it clear what should be included in the system and what should not, as well as what these decisions are based on.	An organization that today uses a process where none of the practices mentioned at left are covered can reach an increase in productivity of up to 30%. If only one of the practices is missing, the increase tends to be 10–15% when adopting RUP.
Use of software tools	It is a good practice to adopt RUP and tools to support the developers' work in parallel.	By automating time-consuming tasks, providing integration between the members of the project, and so on, productivity can be raised by 15–30%.
Architecture and risk resolution	Architecture is implemented early in the project in order to verify the technical solution and reduce the technical risks. A component-based architecture reusing proven patterns is used. RUP is architecture centric; much of the other work according to the process is derived from the architecture.	By going from a waterfall process driven by documentation to an architecture-first approach driven by risk resolution, the productivity can be expected to increase by 5%.
Team cohesion	Using RUP as a common language improves communication, minimizes misunderstanding, and leads to less need for rework.	The value of improving this parameter grows with the size of the project, but a productivity increase of 5% is reasonable to expect.
Process maturity	Adoption of RUP provides an integrated process that focuses on the end product. (Note the importance of an *integrated* process. Introducing a process that covers a single area only can in some cases decrease the productivity.)	The benefit of creating an integrated process can be expected to raise the productivity by 5%. But note that a poor adoption of RUP, where people are not trained and supported enough, will not increase your productivity. It might even have the opposite effect.

Table 5.1   *COCOMO II Parameters Dependent on Process Used*

If the long-term improvement in productivity can be expected to be 30%, each project after the pilot will save 30% of $1,020,000 ($306,000), which means that the break-even point will be reached during the project after the pilot.[1]

Let us take the example a bit further. We already discussed different ways to reduce the productivity dip. Some of these might be hard to do when people aren't experienced in working with change or in RUP itself. Moreover, during an adoption the main challenge may be to learn the new process while still delivering good software. If a *mentor* is used to help reduce the dip, an extra cost is introduced. But normally the benefits of having a mentor cover that cost by reducing the cost of the dip and increasing the long-term benefits of the process.

Assume that a mentor works on the pilot project an average of 2 days a week during the first 5 months (2 days/week × 4 weeks/month × 5 months = 40 days) and that the company pays $2,000/day for the mentor. This adds to the pilot project investment an extra cost of 40 days × $2,000/day = $80,000. The mentor, however, helps reduce the productivity dip to be just 5% instead of 20% and increases the long-term productivity to be 40% instead of 30%. Now the initial cost of the pilot project is .05 × $1,020,000 + $30,000 (licenses and training) + $80,000 (mentoring) = $161,000. Each project after the pilot will now save .40 × $1,020,000 = $408,000, which means that the break-even point will be reached during the project after the pilot.[2] But assuming that the mentor can help the team working on the pilot project increase its productivity during the later stages of the pilot, let's say by half of the long-term expectations of $408,000 (i.e., $204,000), the break-even point will be reached during the pilot itself.[3]

5.1.4 Other Aspects to Cover in a Business Case

In addition to the process-related parameters from COCOMO II discussed earlier, when creating the business case you should consider some other aspects related to the people in the organization:

---

1. The cost of two average projects not using RUP: $1,020,000$_{proj1}$ + $1,020,000$_{proj2}$ = $2,040,000. The cost of two projects with RUP introduced in the first one and RUP used in the second one: ($1,020,000 + $234,000)$_{proj1}$ + ($1,020,000 − $306,000)$_{proj2}$ = $1,968,000. Gain: $2,040,000 − $1,968,000 = $72,000.
2. The cost of two projects with RUP introduced by a RUP mentor in the first one and RUP used in the second one: ($1,020,000 + $161,000)$_{proj1}$ + ($1,020,000 − $408,000)$_{proj2}$ = $1,793,000. Gain: $2,040,000 − $1,793,000 = $247,000.
3. The cost of a project with RUP introduced by a RUP mentor and where the project experiences a productivity increase already in its later stages: $1,020,000 + $161,000 − $204,000 = $977,000. Gain: $1,020,000 − $977,000 = $43,000.

- The capabilities of the analysts, developers, and testers
- Personnel experience
- Personnel continuity

These tend to be difficult to measure in dollars, but at least personnel continuity might be worth considering when making business case calculations. Keep in mind the costs of recruiting new employees compared with the costs of retaining personnel.

5.2   Motivating the People

Here we bring up a few factors shown to be important to consider when implementing a new process in an organization. If these factors are given proper attention, the implementation will be significantly easier to complete. In contrast, if one or more of these factors are forgotten, the implementation and its positive effects will be jeopardized. This discussion is not intended to be complete; we just want to point out some important factors that unfortunately are forgotten or underestimated very often. Who will make the change happen? The people in the organization! Your ability to guide people through the change will have a high impact on the results of your process implementation.

5.2.1   Reactions to Change

When an individual or a group of individuals (e.g., a department, a project team) is exposed to a change, you can expect some reactions. One very natural reaction when facing a change is resistance or avoidance. If such reactions are not dealt with, by the leaders of the change or by any of the "change agents" (e.g., the RUP mentors), the change—in our case, the implementation of a new process—will be delayed or might even fail completely.

What reactions can we expect from people going through a change? The internationally recognized psychologist Claes Janssen[4] [1996] has developed one of many theories in this area. The theory known as the *Four Rooms of Change* defines four "rooms" people can inhabit during a change (see Figure 5.3). Each room represents what *feelings* the individual has toward the change and what *behavior* we can expect from him or her.

---

4. See his Web site at http://www.claesjanssen.com.

Figure 5.3   *The theory of the Four Rooms of Change, defined by Claes F. Janssen. Starting at the upper left and moving counterclockwise, the rooms are contentment, denial, confusion, and renewal.*

Contentment People feel "at home"—they know all the tasks they're expected to perform and are satisfied with the situation. (But they do not necessarily see the situation as optimal.) People are usually in the *contentment room* before the change starts. When they hear about the change, through the first information meetings, they usually move into the *denial room*.

Denial People are exposed to the change but have not committed to it. Hesitation and criticism can be expected. An often-heard comment is "Yes, I will start to work like that—later." Holding on to the old routines, people deny that the change will affect them.

People who are in the denial room are not receptive to information and training. The mentor (or other change agents) needs to focus on showing successful examples of the new process. When it comes to management commitment, we have never seen a company where the managers have not told us that they support the implementation of RUP. However, we have seen several companies where they have not "lived the commitment."

When events occur that complicate the overall situation in the company, the change project loses priority. Experience tells us that it is hard to restart an implementation effort that has been placed on hold. In the denial room, it is essential that management stay firm, showing a determination to go through with the change.

When it becomes obvious that the change is happening, people usually move into the *confusion room*.

Confusion People start to realize that things are changing whether they like it or not. Feelings like frustration, confusion, helplessness, and fear emerge. It is common to begin to see benefits from the change in one moment and in the next to feel doubt that the change is the right thing to pursue.

It should be easy to perform day-to-day work according to the suggested process, or at least easy to understand how the tasks should be performed. It is important to create a "not harder than this?" feeling among the employees and guide them smoothly into the new process by comparing the new tasks with tasks they perform today. If you succeed in this, people will get more and more positive about the change. Watch for silence—that is often a sign of growing resistance to the process. People who react in this way often hope that if they ignore the change, they will be able to perform their work in "the old way" in the future as well. Most of the work within software development today is performed to a large extent in teams. This means everyone must change, or nothing will change!

The more negative attitudes there are toward the change, the harder you need to work to address the questions of the people involved. One of the most effective steps is to involve as many of the skeptics as possible in the implementation work. Involvement creates commitment and manageable attitudes.

In the confusion room people feel the need for (and are also more receptive to) more information, so now is a good time to start training a broader range of people. Training can be done in several different ways, including traditional classroom training, Web-based self-studies, books, workshops, and on-the-job training with a mentor. All types of training are more or less suitable depending on the situation and individual needs. Make sure that you use a variety of learning methods and that you know the individuals' training needs, both in content and time. Timing is crucial; all experience shows that individuals benefit more from the training if it is done close to when the knowledge can be applied to real work. This is known as just-in-time training.

Finally, when people overcome their fears and worries about the change, they move into the renewal room.

Renewal The benefits of the change are visible, and people start to feel insightful, competent, and ecstatic about their work.

5.2.2 Keep Moving between the Four Rooms of Change

No change will happen if people stay in the contentment room, so you need to move them out of there. Once they move to the next room, denial, it is important to keep them moving in order to *avoid losing productivity* in the organization (see Figure 5.4).

People tend to stay longer in the denial room if they feel that someone else pushes the change on them. Therefore, a substantial effort needs to be spent on communicating with the people who will be affected by the process implementation to ensure that they understand why the change is needed and what the organization wants to achieve (the goals).

A common mistake is to have a small group of people from top management and process management evaluate the situation and the process to be implemented for several months before telling anyone else in the company. In this situation, the members of the small group move between the rooms. When they reach the renewal room, they are very enthusiastic about the process and start the implementation of it. The rest of the company then moves into the denial room and after a while (hopefully) to the confusion room. So a small group of *enthusiastic* people is talking to a large group of *confused* people who are not yet ready to listen because they have not worked out their views and feelings of the proposed change! The implementation effort benefits from having as big a part of the organization as possible moving between the rooms as a coherent group. Even if it is impossible to reach this ideal completely, it is important to strive for it.

As always, recognize that individuals are different. People move between the rooms at different speeds. Make sure to give each individual the right support during the change process. Read more about how to tailor communication to different needs in Chapter 6, "Planning the RUP Adoption."

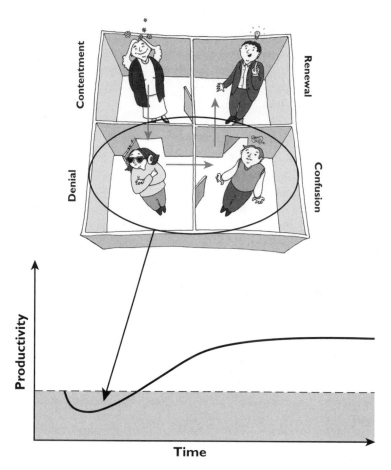

Figure 5.4   *In the denial and confusion rooms, people tend to be less productive than in the contentment and renewal rooms.*

5.3   Following Up the Business Case and People's Attitudes

Before a process implementation begins, goals for the effort (i.e., adoption goals) should be stated for the organization. These should be measurable in the context of the organization (and connected to the business case described above). This means that during the implementation it should be possible to judge whether the implementation is on track or not. That is, it should be possible to *collect measurements* or data from "the real world"

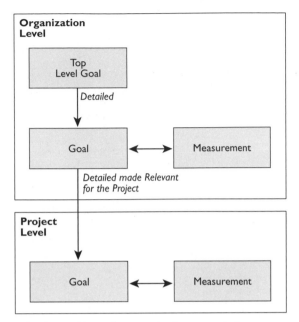

Figure 5.5   *Goals for the organization and its projects need to be connected.*

during the implementation to be used to judge whether the goals have been fulfilled or not. For each software development project team that takes part in the process implementation by using parts of the process, goals connected to the implementation effort should be stated as well (i.e., project adoption goals). These goals should be more detailed than the ones on the organization level in order to be relevant to the project. Another set of measurements needs to be defined for these goals, and the follow-up of these should be more frequent—once per phase in RUP or even once per iteration. Figure 5.5 summarizes the relationships between organization and project goals.

A common *problem with goals* is that even if they are very relevant to the organization and the projects, they *do not affect the way people work every day.* For instance, if the organization stated a goal to increase productivity by 20% in two years, progress toward that goal can be measured and followed up after two years, and we will know whether it was reached or not. But will people really feel urgency due to that goal? Probably not. For that to happen, team or individual goals that are relevant in day-to-day work and that will have a positive impact on the goals on the organization level need to be stated.

At the European Software Institute (ESI), the work of the Balanced IT Scorecard [Reo et al. 1999] has been developed to adapt the concepts of the Balanced Scorecard [Kaplan and Norton 1996] to connect the top-level goals in an organization with software process improvement initiatives. ESI suggests that four elements can be used when monitoring a process implementation:

- *Goals* are quantitative statements of what must be achieved and when it must be achieved.
- *Lag indicators* (connected to the goals) are measurements that can determine whether progress is lagging behind what was expected and to what degree the goal is or is not being achieved.
- *Drivers* (connected to the goals) are factors that positively affect the achievement of established goals.
- *Lead indicators* (connected to the drivers) are measurements of how well the drivers perform and how well they support the goals' achievement.

Using the elements above, let us take an example using a sample goal.

- *Goal:* Productivity should be increased by 20% after two years.
- *Lag indicator:* Increases in the cost per source line of code in a project indicate that the progress toward the goal is lagging.
- *Driver:* Problem analysis and requirements need to be agreed upon by all stakeholders.
- *Lead indicator:* Increases in the number of change requests due to an inability to capture initial requirements indicate that the progress toward the driver is not acceptable.

Normally it is possible to find more than one driver for a goal.

If we expand on the concepts from ESI, using the above-mentioned elements, it is possible to combine the ideas regarding goals and measurements for both the organizational and project levels. The goal and the lag indicator are considered on the organization level. Drivers and lead indicators are defined for each development project. In this way the drivers become goals for the project. This method ensures that the process-related goals for a development project are aligned with the goals for the overall process implementation effort, (see Figure 5.6).

It has become more and more popular to use *assessment frameworks* like the Capability Maturity Model (CMM) created by Carnegie Mellon University

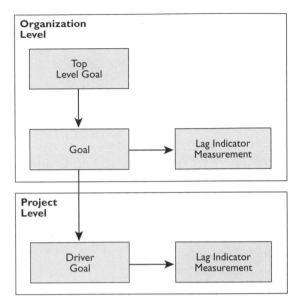

Figure 5.6   *Mapping the concepts, Driver, Lag Indicator and Lead Indicator, from ESI to goals for an organization and its projects*

[1995] or the more flexible CMMi and ISO/IEC 15504, commonly known as SPICE,[5] to follow up the effects of a process improvement. The CMM is used to guide internal software process improvement activities and to assess the underlying principles for software process maturity. SPICE is a major international initiative to support the development of an international standard for process assessment. In short, the process is examined by an assessment, and the results from the assessments are used both to determine the capability of the organization and to initiate process improvements.

Finally, do not forget that many of the factors that will cause the implementation to succeed or fail are *nontechnical*. People who use the new process and do not feel happy about the new way of working can cause it to fail. We recommend defining goals and measurements for the human aspects of the implementation as well. One way to measure people's experiences with and attitudes toward the implementation is to use a *questionnaire*. You can find more about this in Chapter 7, "Obtaining Support from the Organization," where you will also find examples of questions to ask.

---

5. Software Process Improvement and Capability dEtermination; see http://www.sqi.gu.edu.au/spice/.

5.4   Examples of Goals and Measurements

Table 5.2 shows four examples of how goals, lag indicators, drivers, and lead indicators can look when used on a process adoption project.

Organization level		Project Level	
Goal	**Lag Indicator**	**Driver**	**Lead Indicator**
Productivity shall be increased by 20% in two years.	Cost per source line of code in a project	Problem analysis and requirements need to be agreed upon by all stakeholders.	Number of change requests due to the inability to capture initial requirements
The market position shall be sustained due to a more professional way of working.	Regular measurements of market share	Increase the average SPICE rating for projects.	Results from SPICE assessments
Time-to-market shall be improved by 15% in three years.	Average calendar time to complete a new product version	Calendar time per source line of code should decrease compared with the last project.	Accuracy of schedule compared to plan when passing milestones
Job satisfaction among individuals shall increase.	Results from questionnaires	People must be motivated through possibilities for personal growth.	Number of employees who take on new responsibilities in the project

Table 5.2   *Examples of Goals, Lag Indicators, Drivers, and Lead Indicators*

5.5   Conclusion

To obtain long-lasting support for the adoption, it has to be well motivated. It has to be possible to see the return on investment so that management and the employees feel the urgent need to improve and will do their very best to go through the (at times) uncomfortable change. You should also have the ambition to follow up the effects of the change to see that you benefit from it and stay on track.

In the next chapter, we will help you structure the adoption and plan for it.

6

Planning the RUP Adoption

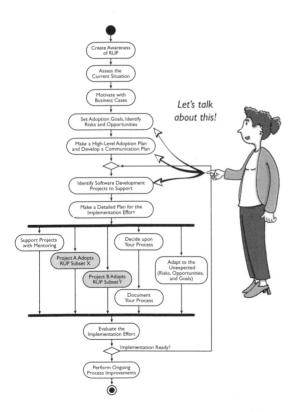

Let's talk about this!

The motivations are clear. You know that your organization will benefit from adopting RUP. You know that if you can get each and every person to practice RUP when engaged in software development, the adoption will succeed and your goal will be reached. But how can that be done? We know from earlier initiatives of implementing RUP across organizations that just making RUP available and letting people "help themselves" won't work. Forcing people won't work either, and making the process tempting to people won't work by itself. Instead you should *help people* and—even better—*plan how you will help them*. The help includes defining suitable RUP subsets for different projects to start from, setting up infrastructure that enables people to share experiences along the way, and many more "adoption activities" that, if followed, will lead you to your goal.

Remember your imagined hike in the beginning of Chapter 4? You liked the berries in the forest so much that you got lost. Well, you have now found where you are on the map, and the goal is still marked with an X. You can use the compass to determine which direction to move in. But now there's a new problem: There is a swamp in the way, and beyond the swamp, toward your goal, the forest is rather thick. You cannot see the goal itself, but you can see a big rock on the other side of the swamp. You can find the rock easily on your map, and although it is not along the straight path to the goal, it is a known position *much* closer to where you want to go. At the rock you can use the compass to find the direction to the goal once more and look for another visible landmark even closer to the goal. By dividing the long journey into several shorter segments, all of them ending in known positions, you reduce the risk of getting lost again. This has some positive side effects.

- You will not get entangled in the blackberry bushes.
- You can eat all the berries you want as long as you keep track of the next landmark.

You should plan and deal with a process implementation in a similar way. Heading straight for the goal may seem appealing, but it is very risky. Most likely either you'll fail to reach the goal completely or you'll lose speed due to the long-term focus (people tend to treat a short-term goal as more urgent than a long-term goal). Or worse, you might lose some people because the task seems too demanding for them and they give up. What you need is a good *adoption plan*. You also need to put the plan into a document.

Changing some of the more important business processes in an organization affects a lot of people. The simple rules of "one step at a time" (dividing the journey) and "a pat on the back" (celebrating accomplishments) as new accomplishments have been achieved are important. Changes spread across the organization during a period of time, and many different activities need to take place to support the changes. A major change like adopting RUP needs to be planned in a careful way to keep things under control for the following reasons.

- You do not want to get lost.
- You want to keep out of trouble.
- You want to gather benefits along the way.

As described in this chapter, the implementation team does the actual planning and later will be in charge of executing the plan. The planning begins when you detail the business case to help set the adoption goals. To be prepared for sudden events, you should also identify risks and opportunities and plan what to do if they occur. Then you should make a high-level adoption plan that documents your adoption goals along with the major activities you plan to undertake throughout the RUP adoption. Because "it's all about people," you should also develop a communication plan. Most important of all, you should identify potential pilot projects; when you have found these projects, the detailed planning of the implementation can start.

6.1 Creating the Implementation Team

Presumably, up to this point some people in your organization have handled "the RUP issues" (e.g., assessment, creation of a business case, and so on). However, when you begin planning the RUP adoption, the amount of work increases, so we recommend that you put together an *implementation team* whose main task is the RUP adoption. Some organizations prefer delegating the RUP adoption entirely to the software development project teams, but using an organizational implementation team ensures that no redundancy work will take place and provides other valuable benefits for the organizational RUP adoption. Read more about the implementation team in Chapter 7, "Obtaining Support from the Organization."

A trap worth mentioning is the decision to staff the implementation team extensively with external consultants. Although this hopefully brings people experienced in RUP into the organization, there are two major disadvantages. First, the ownership of the process will become unclear to the people in the organization, which adds the risk that the adoption will halt when the consultants leave their assignments. The second disadvantage is the risk that the consultants will be reluctant to transfer enough knowledge to the organization because their assignments will end when the organization is self-sufficient in RUP knowledge. Ideally an implementation team is staffed mainly with the organization's own personnel but supplemented with one or more external RUP mentors, depending on the RUP implementation knowledge and needs among the implementation team members engaged so far.

6.2   Setting Adoption Goals

Your top-level goal of fulfilling the RUP business case (see Chapter 5, "Motivating the RUP Adoption") needs to be detailed in order to be relevant for how the RUP adoption including the implementation will proceed. Why should RUP be implemented? What opportunities might exist? Brainstorming on these questions should result in a list of possible detailed goals. Consider whether each possible goal has a correlation to the business goals of your organization and the RUP business case. If so, it's a relevant goal for the business and for the adoption; let's call it an *adoption goal*. As an example, one possible relevant goal for a telecom operator is "Deliver on time" if one of the business goals is "Always be first out on the market with new services." Since the implementation of RUP could speed up development, "Deliver on time" is also a relevant adoption goal.

It is important to define both *long-term* and *short-term* adoption goals. Intermediate goals help you stay focused and keep the work moving. The goals need to be relevant for the organization, for its projects, and for the individuals on those projects (see "Following Up the Business Case and People's Attitudes" in Chapter 5). It is also good if the goals can be directly tied to the implementation of the new process. For instance, if profitability is used as a basis for a goal, other factors such as market conditions will have a larger impact on the goal than the process will. Evaluation of the process implementation will be difficult with such goals. Still, there is one "not-only-process-related" goal that is mandatory and particularly relevant for the implementation itself:

> *Ensure that every project that uses RUP succeeds.*

If a project fails for some reason (e.g., fails to build the key functionality of the intended system on time, exceeds its budget dramatically, and so on), you can bet that the project members will put RUP on the list of reasons that the project didn't work. No one wants to look bad or point out someone else. But blaming RUP is "harmless." Such a scenario creates ill will for RUP and the implementation.

On the other hand, if a project using RUP succeeds, RUP will get at least part of the credit for it. The heroes of a successful project are, of course, the project members, but it is very likely that RUP has contributed to the success by providing the team with a common language, a sound way to

#	Sample Goal	Refers To
1	Ensure that every project that uses RUP succeeds.	Implementation
2	The number of failed projects (e.g., delayed, beyond budget, missing functionality, poor quality) shall decrease by X% in Y years.	Efficiency
3	The software functionality shall be more aligned with business objectives. *(If possible, express this goal more specifically.)*	Efficiency
4	The market position shall be sustained due to a more professional way of working. *(If possible, express this goal more specifically.)*	Efficiency
5	Time-to-market shall be improved by X% in Y years.	Efficiency
6	Predictability regarding plans and estimates shall be improved. *(If possible, express this goal more specifically.)*	Efficiency
7	Productivity shall increase by X% in Y years.	Efficiency
8	Use cases shall be used for requirements handling.	Process improvement
9	It shall be possible to trace from requirements to testing.	Process improvement
10	Code generation from design models shall be used.	Process improvement
11	A controlled process for handling change requests shall be implemented.	Process improvement
12	The communication between departments A and B shall be improved.	Process improvement
13	Job satisfaction among individuals shall increase.	"Soft" matter
14	Capability (better job performance, personal growth) of individuals shall improve.	"Soft" matter
15	There shall be less confusion and misunderstandings (due to common language, common process).	"Soft" matter
16	At least X% of individuals shall be certified[a] in their discipline (competence area) within Y years.	"Soft" matter
17	Personnel turnover shall decrease by X%.	"Soft" matter
18	It shall become easier to perform job rotation internally.	"Soft" matter
19	Every individual shall have access to RUP.	Implementation
20	Every individual shall have relevant tools installed.	Implementation
21	The organization shall be self-sufficient in RUP expertise within Y years.	Implementation

Table 6.1   *Sample RUP Adoption Goals*

---

[a] Many companies provide customer certifications in various areas. Such a certification may involve attending one or more training sessions, performing some tests, and accruing 5–10 years of practical software development experience.

distribute development efforts over time, and so on. As Grady Booch says, "Good people with a good process will outperform good people with no process every time" [Booch 1996, p. 188]. We claim that even a project canceled early could be regarded as a success if the reason for canceling the project was that, for example, you realized due to a proper problem analysis as described in RUP that you would build software no one wants.

But there are more goals to be set than just making sure projects using RUP succeed. It is good to make goals specific, measurable, attainable, realistic, and tangible, especially if you want to follow up the adoption as described in the related section of Chapter 5. In Table 6.1 we give you some hints on areas for which goals (organization-level as well as project-level goals) can be specified. First, goals can refer to the cost-effectiveness and performance of an organization and its projects. Second, goals can address process-related improvement areas found during the assessment performed earlier. Third, goals can address "soft" matters such as job satisfaction (organizational and individual goals). Finally, like the "Ensure that every project that uses RUP succeeds" goal, some other goals can be tied closely to the implementation of RUP itself.

6.3   Identifying Risks and Opportunities

An awareness of risks is essential when implementing RUP. Risks are anything that may stop us from succeeding with a long-term or short-term goal. The kinds of risks that appear in software development and in process implementation are very different. When running software projects, many risks are technical, such as the risk of not being able to master the technology to build a system that does not exceed the required response times. Naturally, when implementing RUP, most risks are related to human factors—for example, people who need to learn to work in a new way might oppose and hinder the implementation.

We have come across a number of reasons why RUP implementations fail or are delayed. These risks relate to scope, training, tools, and support/mentoring (see Table 6.2). What may be considered as opportunities for the RUP adoption are probably already part of the assessment findings (see Chapter 4, "Assessing Your Organization"). But if any new opportunities arise after the assessment, you may collect these with the risks in a *risk and opportunity list document*.

#	Sample Risk	Refers To
1	The organization tries to adopt too many large chunks of RUP at the same time.	Scope
2	Management has unrealistic expectations regarding scope and time.	Scope
3	The organization is trying to do too many other new things at the same time.	Scope
4	Individuals receive inappropriate training (too much too soon, not enough, or not connected to actual tasks).	Training
5	People participate in use case training or OO training (theoretically differ from RUP) rather than specific RUP training.	Training
6	The process is not supported with appropriate tools.	Tools
7	There is a lack of tool integration: Tool A does not work together with tool B.	Tools
8	There is not enough support from good external mentors.	Support/mentoring
9	There are too few internal mentor candidates to educate the people in the organization.	Support/mentoring
10	The external mentors are not experienced enough ("process lovers" rather than pragmatists).	Support/mentoring
11	The organization allows project teams to adopt RUP on their own.	Support/mentoring
12	The organization tries to support too many projects at the same time.	Support/mentoring
13	There is no proactive support, just late reviews.	Support/mentoring
14	Management does not support the RUP effort enough.	Support/mentoring
15	Key personnel are unwilling to adhere to management decisions.	Support/mentoring

#	Sample Opportunity	Refers To
1	Project A is about to start and the project manager has hired a RUP mentor.	Opportunity
2	The consultants in successful project B will end their assignments soon. (You should collect their experiences before they leave!)	Opportunity
3	After a reorganization, there are some cultural aspects to override. (RUP might be a good choice for a new common language.)	Opportunity

Table 6.2   *Sample Risks and Opportunities*

6.4   Making a High-Level RUP Adoption Plan

In modern iterative software development (as described in RUP), making an excessively detailed plan early in the project is a trap. Things *will* happen that will cause you to change your plan. However, a high-level, rough plan that covers the whole adoption effort is needed in order to communicate how the implementation should proceed. Also, the implementation team must not lose focus or speed and has to stick to long-term goals and a long-term time schedule.

A high-level plan for an adoption should have the following scope:

• The whole organization
• The whole RUP (including selected RUP plug-in extensions)
• All necessary supporting software development tools
• The time period from the start of the adoption (implementation) until it is finished

This scope may be tightened due to the fact that not all parts of the organization would benefit from RUP (e.g., the parts of the organization that don't involve software) or due to the fact that not all of RUP is appropriate in the context of the organization (e.g., there is a well-established deployment process that is "good enough").

The resulting scope is presumably too big to implement in one big chunk. You need to partition the implementation in easy-to-grasp steps. You have to decide the order in which the RUP implementation will proceed. Which parts of the organization benefit most from using RUP? Which projects shall be the first ones to use RUP? Which ones will follow? Will RUP be used when maintaining existing systems not developed with RUP? Which parts of RUP and which tools shall be implemented first? Will different kinds of projects use different parts of RUP, and if so, which parts? What additions need to be made to RUP? Finally, what is the time plan for all of this? (A successful and sustainable "RUP humpchart painting" of your organization requires good preparation work, good tools, and good craftspeople; see Figure 6.1.)

Not all of these questions can be answered now. The detailed planning needs to be performed later. At this point you have guidance for the planning given by:

Figure 6.1 *Plan your work carefully in order for your "RUP humpchart painting" to appeal as well as to last.*

- The assessment findings
- The goals
- The risks (and new opportunities since the assessment was made)

With that input, begin the planning by selecting an overall strategy for the implementation. You will find some possible strategies near the end of this chapter (see "Choosing a Strategy for the RUP Adoption"). In our experiences the most common strategy is the "normal approach," which means start with one to four pilot projects, adopting different parts of RUP in depth. However—as always—which strategy to choose depends on the situation at your organization.

6.4.1   What Should the RUP Adoption Plan Cover?

The high-level plan may encompass the assessment, the establishment of an implementation project or team, the writing and ownership of an organization-wide communication plan, the definition of how to measure the performance of projects, the activities involved when identifying and supporting software development projects that will use RUP, and the establishment of a maintenance team for the final RUP-based organizational process (including development tools).

An implementation plan might be a simple chart defining dates, resources, and durations for the activities. If an implementation team (described in Chapter 7, "Obtaining Support from the Organization") handles the change, the implementation plan will be identical to the project plan for the implementation project.

No matter how the plan is defined, it has to cover the activities for:

- Setting goals
- Selecting which parts of the process to introduce
- Determining when to introduce which part of the process
- Deciding in what order different parts of the organization should be affected
- Deciding what training to deliver and when
- Planning for activities with the purpose of informing the employees
- Assigning roles and responsibilities

These kinds of activities were discussed already in Chapter 1, "How to Adopt RUP in Your Organization," and naturally they appear in your organization's adoption plan. If you put the main high-level RUP adoption activities into a simple table along with some rough target dates, you may end up with something like Table 6.3. (The sample adoption/implementation activities in Table 6.3 assume the "normal approach" strategy discussed briefly above.)

You may also add activities that *support* the process implementation (provide some known landmarks along the way) because it is beneficial to keep everything related to the change together.

- *Certification*: An organization might set goals to have a number of employees pass certain certifications during the implementation by attending one or more training sessions, performing some tests, and so on, depending on what the certifications require. Certifications are

Activity	Deliverables	Time
Assess the organization's current situation	Assessment report	Q1, year 1
Establish the implementation team	—	Q2, year 1
Set goals for the implementation	Implementation plan (goals), opportunity list	Q2, year 1
Identify what can go wrong (risks) and mitigation strategies	Risk list	Q2, year 1
Plan and schedule the implementation	Implementation plan (schedule)	Q2, year 1
Plan communication of the implementation to the organization	Communication plan	Q2, year 1
Identify pilot projects	—	Q3, year 1
Map RUP to existing processes within the organization	Organization-level configuration	Q3, year 1
Plan training of internal mentors	—	Q3, year 1
Plan the pilot projects: • Assess the project's situation • Select appropriate increments of RUP to implement (should be aligned to organizational goals)	Project assessment report, development case (initial version), project implementation plan	Q3, year 1
Develop the RUP platform for the organization-wide process	Web site (initial)	Q3, year 1
Train and execute pilot projects with the first process increment	Development case (updated)	Q3–Q4, year 1
Harvest the pilot projects' experience and populate the RUP platform	Web site (updated with guideline documents, sample project artifacts)	Q1, year 2
Make RUP platform generally available and communicate its purpose and content	—	Q1, year 2
Plan the next stage in detail and update the high-level plan	Risk list (updated), implementation plan (updated), opportunity list (updated)	Q1, year 2
Train, plan, and execute new pilot projects with the next process increment	Documents as above	Q2–Q3, year 2

Table 6.3   *Sample RUP Adoption Activities for an Organization (including hints on their timing)*

not vital to achieve the necessary development competence but can work as extra motivation for the employees. If certifications will be used, they need to be planned in the context of the implementation when is a certain certification needed or desirable?

- *Tools*: In order to reach full productivity in development, tools should be used to automate and support certain tasks. The implementation plan should show when each tool should be installed for what group of developers.

- *Mentoring*: In Chapter 11, "A Guide to Successful Mentoring," we describe our view on how to best benefit from the use of mentors. It feels natural to put into the plan some of the tasks a mentor performs (e.g., workshops, reviews, and so on); it is easy to understand where these fit in among the other activities. But a mentor can be very useful even when not performing tangible activities. Just by "being around" a mentor can accelerate the change among people needed to adapt to the new way of working. Hence, putting in the implementation plan such phrases as "Mentoring around the requirements area two days a week for two months" can be useful.

Finally, having a *special document* that includes scheduled implementation activities and other items offers many advantages. When put into a document, a high-level adoption plan typically encompasses the sections shown in Figure 6.2.

One element that is often forgotten in an implementation plan is the definition of *critical success factors* (e.g., support from management, the ability to identify suitable pilot projects, and so on). It is important to define these and document them in the implementation plan in order to make them visible and to get agreement about them. During the implementation, these success factors need to be monitored and followed up in the same way as project risks.

6.4.2   Why Use a Documented Formal Plan?

Those of you who know your Covey [1990] have heard about "Begin with the end in mind." Thinking through how to get to the goal before acting helps you achieve the desired results. Creating a formal plan forces you to spend time analyzing the problems you may face. By making the plan formal, you actually communicate to the organization that the implementation is a serious effort that will be controlled and monitored.

1. Introduction
   1.1 Purpose and Scope of the Plan
   1.2 Definitions and Acronyms
   1.3 References
2. Executive Summary
   2.1 Business-Level Desired Results (Business Goals)
   2.2 Current Status in the Organization (Assessment Findings)
   2.3 Software Development-Level Desired Results (Adoption Goals)
3. Overview of the Implementation
4. Critical Success Factors
5. Schedule
6. Activities (in detail)

Activity	Deliverables	Time
Assess the organization's current situation	Assessment report	Q1, year 1
Establish implementation team	—	Q2, year 1

7. Deliverables (in detail)
8. Certifications
9. Tools
10. Mentoring
11. Roles and Responsibilities
12. Criteria for Changing the Plan

Figure 6.2   *A sample RUP adoption/implementation plan*

Just as working with an approach like use case modeling helps you find all the requirements when building a system, the activity of writing a plan for the process implementation *helps you find all aspects* that must be considered in order to succeed. Defining on paper what you already have planned in your head causes you to think it all over once more, reviewing the details so you can explain them well and involving other people in order to create acceptance and buy-in for the plan. All this results in a plan of higher quality.

Other side effects have to do with *communication*. A documented implementation plan can be used when communicating with all employees and the different project teams. It will also be easier to keep your momentum toward the goal with the implementation because the goals will be visible through the plan.

6.4.3   On What Level Should Planning Occur?

Whether or not an implementation project will be used, the implementation will benefit from a plan on the organization level. The actual implementation (change), however, takes place in the software development projects, and implementation-related activities need to be in the project plan for each development project as well.

As you saw in Chapter 5, "Motivating the RUP Adoption," as well as earlier in this chapter, we recommend defining goals on both the *organization level* and the *project level* (and preferably also on the individual level). Naturally, the implementation needs to be planned on both levels, including activities leading to the fulfillment of these goals. The metrics will tell whether or not you are on track during the implementation.

We already mentioned that a long-term plan is expected to change sooner or later due to changes in the organization—changes that are out of the control of the process implementation team. The challenges in this kind of situation are to make a detailed enough plan that can accommodate change without too much work and, at the same time, to make the plan relevant for the organization. The same solution used when planning software development iteratively (as described in RUP) applies. First, make a high-level plan for the total adoption, then divide the implementation into several iterations and plan each of those in detail. Making the detailed plan for a shorter period of time lowers the risk of changes. Keeping the long-term plan at a high level reduces the effort needed to update that plan when the environment changes.

Even though the "main" plan will be on the organization level, the implementation will be most visible to the employees through the project plans for the software development projects. Training sessions will appear; new "strangely" named documents and other work products (artifacts) should be produced; there will be new workshops and reviews; and so on.

Planning process implementation activities for a specific development project has other challenges. These activities need to be in the same project plan as the activities that in the end will produce the product (see Figure 6.3). However, there are situations when a separate project implementation plan may be produced (see Chapter 7, "Obtaining Support from the Organization"). This is necessary if the project lacks a docu-

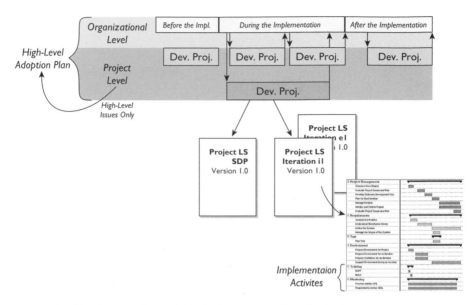

Figure 6.3   *Example of implementation activities in the iteration plan of a development project*

---

mented project plan or if the process needs to be introduced over a period of time that includes a number of (small) projects running one after another. The implementation activities need to have the same priority and be committed to by the project members, especially the project manager who will be responsible for delivering a product and for making sure the project members do their duties.

6.4.4   Who Owns the Plan?

S*omeone in your organization* must own the adoption plan, preferably someone in management or someone appointed by top management. Often an organization has external support at the start of an adoption effort, and it may be tempting to ask the people involved in that external group to write the plan. This might be a trap! There is nothing wrong with getting help when planning the adoption (implementation)—indeed, it is easy to forget things when doing it for the first time—but never give away the ownership of the plan. There is a risk that the implementation will die off if or when the external support ends. There is also a risk that the acceptance of the process will be lower in the organization because "it is not *our* process."

6.5   Developing a Communication Plan

As with all organizational changes, it is very important to communicate to everyone what is happening. We recommend making someone responsible for this task. He or she should document what, how, to whom, and when information regarding RUP and the RUP implementation shall be spread in the organization. This should be done early because people might have questions and worries as a result of the assessment already being made. Figure 6.4 shows a "tool" to use when developing the communication plan, and Figure 6.5 shows a sample communication plan.

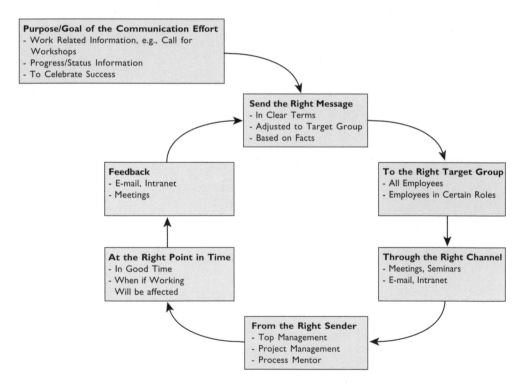

Figure 6.4   *The planning, performance, and evaluation of communication activities*

1. Introduction

1.1 Purpose

To describe how the RUP adoption will be communicated within our organization. The communication aims to support and facilitate the change from the current way of working to the way RUP prescribes. The information shall be coherent, easy to understand, and immediate.

1.2 Scope

Covers important stakeholders for the RUP adoption, their expected involvement levels, and possible communication channels, as well as planned information. Internal communication within the RUP implementation team is not covered, nor is the daily communication between the RUP mentor and his/her pilot project members.

1.3 Definitions and Acronyms

1.4 References

Ref 1   RUP Adoption Plan
Ref 2   RUP Web Site

2. Stakeholders (Target Groups)

- All personnel
- All personnel managers
- All project managers
- CEO, top management
- System developers, new systems
- System developers, maintenance
- System management
- Security center
- Help desk
- The standardized architecture group
- The quality assurance group
- The database administration network
- The usability test network

3. Communication Channels

3.1 Information Channels

- Our spring/fall kickoff meeting
- Our monthly department information meetings
- The weekly project meetings
- Management meetings
- Steering committee meetings
- Seminars about RUP (the change, the adoption)
- Meetings for exchange of RUP experiences
- Our intranet (our extra "shell" to RUP, RUP itself, the daily news on our organization's home site)
- Our internal magazine
- E-mail
- (RUP workshops, RUP mentors)

3.2 Feedback Channels

All channels above should provide opportunities for dialog and feedback whenever possible. We will also send out a questionnaire to all projects adopting RUP in order to collect opinions and feedback (RUP mentors supporting pilot projects).

...

6. Communication Matrix

Sorts out what information each stakeholder will need.
Expected involvement levels: "Aware of," "Understands," "Accepts," or "Participates."

Stakeholder	Information	Channel	Sender	Involvement Level
All personnel	What RUP is	Seminars	The RUP implementation team	Awareness of
				Participates
All project managers	Management of RUP projects	Seminars, meetings for exchange of RUP experiences	The RUP implementation project manager	
				Understands
CEO	Why RUP, the changed development cycle	Steering committee meetings, management meetings	The RUP implementation project manager, development project manager	
...	...	...	...	...

(continues)

Figure 6.5   *Extract of a sample communication plan*

7. Communication Log
Shows planned as well as already performed activities.

Event	Time	Duration	Feedback	Status
Luncheon seminar "What is RUP" at our canteen	2nd month, year 1	1 hour	Questions & answers	Meeting request sent out 1st month, year 1
. . .	. . .	. . .	. . .	. . .

Figure 6.5   *Extract of a sample communication plan (continued)*

6.6   Identifying Software Development Projects to Support

We have stated that the real implementation of RUP happens on the project level, which means that the real implementation of RUP *starts* within the first supported software development projects—the pilot projects. When making a considerable change, it is very important that the beginning of the change sets off well. Therefore, the pilot projects are critical—it is important to choose pilot projects that are suitable for RUP and will succeed.

What is a good *pilot project?* Below is a list of things to consider if you are in the desired situation of being able to choose among several projects. If supporting more than one project at a time, you should consider the possibility of having separate projects adopt different increments of RUP, which speeds up the implementation and avoids overlapping work. For example, the work on the second project can be easier if you are writing use cases for a particular domain because you can look at the resulting use cases from the first project and reuse the use case model guidelines. You should also consider the possibility of trying out RUP in different kinds of projects, for example, projects developing very different kinds of systems.

1. A pilot project should be representative of the types of projects the organization typically develops; this makes the experiences more relevant to future projects. The project should explore, try, adapt, and adopt parts of RUP that will become "RUP basics" for many other projects to follow. If RUP is going to be used within two different areas of the organization that have different needs (e.g., "new development" and "maintenance"), one pilot project within each area is needed.

2. A pilot project must have reasonably high priority and be reasonably important to the organization. If so, we expect that the project will be staffed with competent people. Also, we expect the project to last, even if it will be necessary to perform cost reductions within the organization. Though a pilot needs to be critical, the situation should not be that the company will go bankrupt if the project fails. The pilot should be a real project, not a contrived project created only to test the process or tools, because such a project will never get the focus needed to be able to succeed with the implementation activities.

3. If the organization is geographically spread out, it is good to spread out the pilot projects to some extent as well. Then RUP "comes closer" to everybody, and the informal communication channels open up (e.g., "talking RUP" with someone you happen to meet at the coffee machine).

4. There should be a general interest among the project members, especially the project manager, in implementing RUP.

5. The project should not try too many other new things at once. The project should not be a pilot for anything but RUP.

6. The timing of the project is important. The RUP implementation in general has a time limit set up in its rough schedule, and pilot projects need to fit within that schedule. If no projects will be started in the near future, the schedule for the implementation needs to be postponed. (In case maintenance on and evolution of existing systems takes place, RUP can, of course, still be implemented.) Moreover, pilot projects should be long enough to prove that the process improvements will work but not so prolonged that they delay the spread of RUP knowledge within the organization.

6.7   Choosing a Strategy for the RUP Adoption

Before planning what kinds of activities should be performed to support your organization's adoption of RUP, you should select an overall strategy that suits your organization. Below we discuss some possible overall strategies.

6.7.1   Wide and Shallow or Narrow and Deep?

Should all of RUP (or the subset you have chosen) be implemented on a basic level at once, or should smaller parts of the process be thoroughly implemented one after the other in several steps? Let us visualize these concepts (see Figure 6.6).

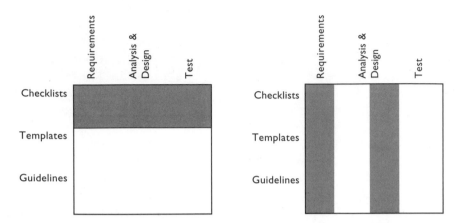

Figure 6.6   *In the wide and shallow approach (left), many disciplines in RUP are considered but only to a certain level of detail. In the narrow and deep approach (right), only a few disciplines are implemented but on a more complete level.*

The bigger the organization and the more of RUP to be implemented, the more likely it is that the narrow and deep approach will prove to be more effective. Let us explore two examples.

- **No urgency:** A company with 100+ developers has been in business for 30 years. The company has a process already but it is not widely used anymore because it has not been updated lately. The company has created mainly software systems developed in the C programming language (a non-OO language) and is not used to iterative development. Recently a number of newly hired employees developed an add-on to an existing system in Java, partly because they knew that language better from school and partly because it was better suited to create a Web interface. The interface to the legacy systems, however, proved to be difficult. Management has talked to other companies in the industry, evaluated RUP, and finally decided to implement just about all of RUP in the organization.

  What strategy should this company use?

  This company is in the middle of a change whether the managers and employees like it or not. The world moves on, technology changes, new media are introduced by the marketplace. Still, the company has older, fully functional software that cannot be replaced (due to time and economic reasons; there is rarely a good argument for rewriting software that works today just because there are newer technologies on the

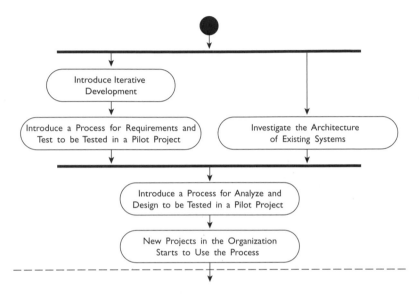

Figure 6.7   *In an organization that has a working process today and is in no real hurry to change, the implementation can be done in several steps with pilot projects doing narrow and deep activities in between.*

market). As a result, the new process should be introduced carefully. This organization knows how to develop software, and there is no real urgency to change the way it works. A narrow and deep approach can be used. Figure 6.7 shows an example of recommended steps.

• **Real urgency:** This time we visit a company that has existed for just a few years. The core of the company was formed by a few old university friends who, after a reunion, started to talk about an idea for a new business and eventually created a company. During the first year the company focused on developing a business case for the product, finding venture capital, proving the basic ideas behind the product, and so on. Now the company has three customers that have a version 1.0 release of the product. The company has grown and employs ten developers. The situation today is rather hectic—the customers, who are not very happy with the software, call almost daily with complaints and requests for enhancements. The person who happens to answer a particular call

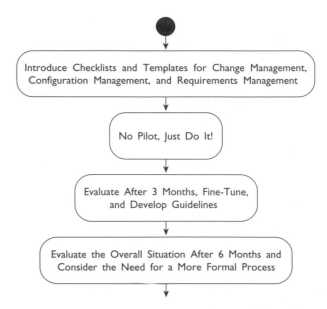

Figure 6.8   *In a small organization that plans to implement only parts of RUP with a wide and shallow approach, all parts can be implemented at once. Make sure to evaluate and reconsider the implementation after a period of time.*

usually produces a fix and e-mails it to the customer. Soon enough the company has no control over which customer has what patch installed. At the same time, the venture capitalists ask when the company will become profitable and recommend an expanded customer base to generate more revenue to justify the expenses.

What strategy should this company use?

First of all, this situation is far more urgent than the first one. The company needs to quickly get control over its installed base and the procedures for handling complaints and additional requirements. The organization's problems are not really related to project work but to the whole organization. Our recommendation would be to use a wide and shallow approach that might look like Figure 6.8.

6.7.2   Just One Project at a Time or the Whole Organization at Once?

Should you initially work out your RUP adaptation in just one project, thereafter spreading the use of RUP to more projects after the pilot has been completed, or should you start several parallel projects, trying out different parts of the process in each one? There are several strategies to choose from here, and no one is superior to the others; it all comes back to the situation the organization is facing. Factors that come into play include the following: Are there several different technology areas in the company where development is done under different constraints? How many potential mentors are available? (These people could give support to the projects.) What are the size and geographical distribution of the organization? Let us investigate two examples and recommended strategies for each one.

- **Single domain:**[1] A company with 100 developers who all work within the same domain plans to implement RUP. These developers have no prior knowledge of RUP, but they are very skilled people. A few developers in the company have a good understanding of the domain and are well known and seen as competent when it comes to choosing design strategies and similar tasks. Management decides that all chosen parts of RUP should be implemented at once.

  What strategy should this company use?

  Here a strategy that is often referred to as the "normal approach" (briefly mentioned earlier in this chapter; also see RUP) is suitable. Under this strategy, one pilot project staffed with the experts as well as some junior employees is started while the rest of the company continues as before.[2] When the first project is completed, the process is evaluated and refined if needed. After that, a couple of new projects using the same process are begun (see Figure 6.9). Experts who took part in the first project support the new projects with experience from using the process. The number of new projects that can be started depends on the number of mentors available. One or more of the experts might be able and willing to act as mentors in the future. Remember that being a great developer is not the same as being a good mentor. Besides the technical skills needed to be a developer, a mentor needs social skills and experience with how people react to change. To become mentors, the individuals will need special coaching (see Chapter 7, "Obtaining Support from the Organization").

---

1. As defined in the RUP Glossary by IBM Rational Software: "Domain: an area of knowledge or activity characterized by a set of concepts and terminology understood by practitioners in that area."
2. A company with 200–300 developers could use 3–4 pilot projects.

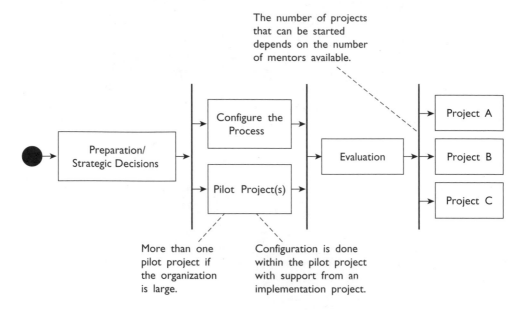

Figure 6.9   *In the "normal approach," a pilot project tries out the process, is evaluated, and if successful is then spread to a number of projects. A good rule of thumb is to start no more than three new projects. Experience shows that a typical organization will have problems supporting all projects if more than three new projects are started after the first one is completed.*

- **Multiple domains:** A company is in the outsourcing business. Its customers do not want to do their software development themselves, so instead they hand off a collection of requirements to this supplier. The company has two big customers, one in the defense area and one that sells trading systems to stock exchanges.

    What strategy should this company use?

    In this situation, the company most likely needs two configurations of RUP. There will be a common base but also some major differences. The "defense branch" will have to focus on how to develop high-performance, real-time systems, and the "trading system branch" will face the challenge of multiple sources of requirements. One solution is to make a high-level configuration to be used by both branches of the company (see Figure 6.10). This will ensure that the organization gets a common language and that certain concepts are understood in the same way. Each branch will do its own implementation of different configurations of the process (using a strategy as in

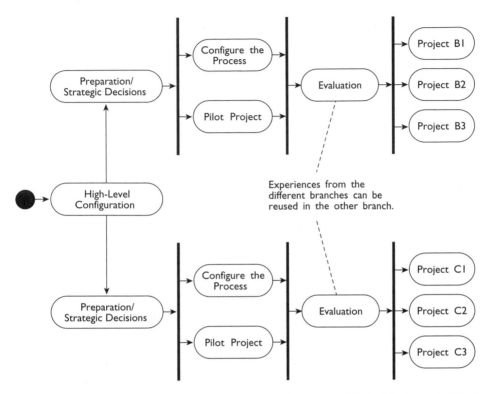

Figure 6.10   *When working in two distinctive areas, two configurations of RUP might be needed. Each configuration should have its own pilot. Experiences from one pilot can be reused in the other configuration and vice versa.*

the single domain example). The separate branches can reuse experiences from each other as time passes, but most likely the processes will diverge more and more.

6.7.3   How Much Time?

If it takes two to three years to fully implement RUP in an organization with 100–200 developers, can it be done in a few months in an organization that has just 10–20 developers? Probably not. If you have chosen the "one project at a time" approach, if the duration of a typical project is six months, and if the project is staffed with 5 developers, it will take you at least a year. It is common to underestimate the time needed to implement a process in an organization. Many things need to be taken into consideration:

- Establishing a common understanding of the need for the change and how to work in the future
- Distributing to the employees information about how the RUP adoption proceeds
- Training for different roles
- Tailoring and customizing RUP for the organization
- Selecting and running pilot projects
- Allowing time needed to "change the view of development" among the employees
- Evaluating results from pilot projects
- Refining the RUP customization

All of these activities take time. If you want to shorten the time for implementation, you must introduce the process in parallel projects. However, this requires a more controlled implementation effort and more extensive use of external mentors. Even when many mentors are used, the time for the implementation cannot be reduced too much. *People need a certain amount of time to adapt to the new ideas,* think about how they will be affected, learn their new (or changed) tasks, and so on. After each step in the change, the organization needs some time to reflect over the change and gain strength to take the next step.

6.8   Conclusion

Planning starts with defining the goals based on the assessment. It is important to identify risks that may hinder the success of the RUP adoption. Plans need to be made both for the long-term change and for each of its steps. Keep the main plan on a level high enough to maintain flexibility, and save the details for the short-term plans that will be developed continuously. Do not forget about communication—plan for it. A documented plan is easier to communicate, so do not keep everything in your head. If you can choose which project to start the adoption with, look for typical projects in your organization that offer experiences relevant for many others in the organization. Depending on your situation, a few different strategies can be followed during the rollout.

In the next chapter, we will discuss the necessary support an organization should give to its development projects to ensure their success during the adoption.

Obtaining Support from the Organization

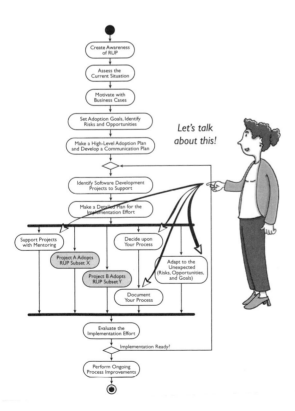

Let's talk about this!

In this chapter we walk you through several of the activities that need to take place in order to make the adoption of RUP happen. To be precise, we discuss activities that need to be done in the organization to support its development projects. We start with a discussion about the need for an implementation team to coordinate the project support. Then we present four steps to perform when supporting each development project. After that we dig into how to harvest experiences, how to communicate, and how to provide support through training, workshops, and reviews. The chapter ends with a description of how an organization can become self-sufficient by training its own employees to give mentor support during an adoption of a new process.

7.1   The Implementation Team and Project

Who in the organization should be responsible for supporting the development projects? As we discussed in Chapter 6, the workload related to the adoption will increase when the plan for the actual roll-out is created. In order to avoid having different development project teams create the same or similar process material from scratch, we recommend centralizing parts of the adoption work to one team of people, the *implementation team*. Organizations that already have a process support team can probably use that team as a good central point for the adoption work.

The implementation team may consist of a project manager, one or more external RUP mentors, a number of internal coworkers performing RUP mentoring, a couple of tool specialists, and perhaps a Web master. The help from mentors is vital in many situations. You need individuals who can assist the project members in working according to the new process. We are firmly convinced that the use of an external mentor in the beginning of an implementation shortens the time needed to get to the goal. An external mentor can also be used to train internal mentors. You will find more about this near the end of this chapter.

We even recommend using *a separate implementation project*, mainly because this makes it easier to control the cost of the RUP implementation and easier to follow it up, plus it takes a lot of pressure off the development project teams. If the implementation project is funded by the organization as a whole, it is easy to separate the cost for the implementation from the cost for the product development. It also becomes easier for the development project teams to accept the use of a RUP mentor when they're not being forced to carry an extra cost.

However, there are still dangers associated with separate implementation projects. It is very important to keep the implementation project focused on implementing processes for the separate development projects! We have seen cases when the implementation project wasn't flexible and supportive enough and therefore hindered self-motivated development projects.

7.2   Supporting Projects When Adopting a RUP Subset

This is the crucial part of the implementation—the projects and the support they are given in order to successfully use an appropriate part of RUP and related tools.

The organization should be prepared to support each development project by following the four steps listed below.

1. **Assess the project.**
   RUP mentors (or assessors) look into the characteristics of the project and find out how the project team members usually develop software and what the most urgent process needs are.

2. **Select from RUP and plan.**
   RUP mentors help the project team choose a relevant subset from RUP to implement, focusing on areas where the need for a process (method) is substantial. The project assessment gives the basic facts. The organization makes sure that the adoption of RUP in the specific project stays in line with overall process implementation goals.

3. **Provide support during the project.**
   The project begins, and RUP mentors give support on all RUP-related activities along the way. The support is sometimes provided individually to project team members acting in a certain RUP role and sometimes to a group of people (e.g., a workshop on how to perform use case modeling).

4. **Spread RUP experiences to other projects.**
   Experiences gained in the development projects are shared with others within the organization. This is done through the organization's RUP adaptation Web site, which is probably on the intranet. Guideline documents, specializations, and customizations of various RUP activities are shared.

These activities are described from the perspective of the project (rather than the organization) in Chapter 8, "How to Adopt RUP in Your Project."

7.3   Harvesting Experiences and Updating the Organization's RUP Adaptation

In parallel with running software development projects, the RUP configuration (tailoring and customization) that the projects use is defined and documented. But shouldn't the configuration be delivered by the organization at the beginning of the project? Not necessarily. At the start of the first projects to implement RUP (the pilot projects), there is a high-level description of the process to be used (based on strategic decisions, the type of development, the type of organization, and so on). After a few steps of the implementation, some reusable experiences and material from previous projects are available. But the final, detailed process for a particular software development project needs to be defined in the project itself.

The main task for the organization is to harvest the experiences of each development project and update the organization's adaptation based on these, making the experiences (in the form of guidelines, checklists, templates, examples, and so on) available for future projects. New development projects will have a more and more complete adaptation to start from (which is *proven* in the organization). We do not recommend that organizations complete their organization-level RUP configurations before running projects. Neither do we recommend that project teams complete their project-level RUP configurations too early. Of course, there will be ideas and "drafts" of how the process will look. But because the main purpose of the project is to deliver software, that work must not be postponed by detailed process configuration activities up front. The organization needs to monitor this and urge the project team to get going.

It is not uncommon that the management wants to see some results from the implementation after each step before committing resources and money to the next step. If you have chosen a more formal method of measuring the capability of the organization, this is the time to perform a measurement to assess how close to the goal the implementation is at the moment. If no formal method is used, the project teams should still be assessed regarding their views of the process and the project's performance. At a minimum, the project members should be given a questionnaire that covers the areas described in Figure 7.1.

Background information

- *Your role and responsibilities in the project*

- *Previous experiences with RUP*

- *Experiences with tools (level of integration, benefits, general experiences)*

- *Your experiences of the maturity of software development in your organization*

How was the adoption of RUP handled?

- *Attitude goals level of communication*

- *Training (Was it suitable for your situation? What could have been done different?)*

- *Mentoring (Was it suitable for your situation? What could have been done different?)*

The effects of RUP

- *How has the productivity been improved?*

- *Does RUP help you in your day-to-day work?*

- *Have quality, communication, traceability, etc. been improved?*

- *Has communication with parties outside the project (customers, production, etc.) been improved?*

- *(If tools were introduced) Have the new tools improved the project's working conditions?*

Figure 7.1 *Some areas to cover in a questionnaire intended to gather RUP adoption feedback*

After each implementation step, the risk list created earlier needs to be revised. Some of the initial risks have probably been taken care of or have disappeared in other ways. Some new risks might have come up. It's also possible (although unlikely) that the list remains intact after an implementation step. The main issue is to be continuously aware of the risks. A change in the risk situation might call for updates in the plans and might even cause you to change your mind about which projects should use the RUP adoption in the next step.

The goals might also change at this point. Even if there is no need to change the goals, you might need to make the goals more detailed and more connected to the projects being run. A goal such as "Time-to-market shall be improved" does not give the project much guidance; a short-term, more detailed goal is needed.

7.4 Documenting Your Project Implementation Plan

Even if the members of your different development project teams have not asked for support (or have not even realized the need for and availability of help), help should be provided. The kinds of support the organization should plan to give can be divided into the following areas:

- Information
- Courses and training
- Start-up workshops
- Artifact reviews
- Milestone reviews
- Individual face-to-face support
- Ad hoc support, that is, support that cannot be planned for

(See also Figure 8.3 in Chapter 8.)

The implementation team in the organization needs to help each development project team plan for these activities. One alternative is to include the activities in the project's normal software development plan (SDP), showing the adoption-related activities together with the development-related activities.

Alternatively, you may choose to keep the SDP free from detailed process and tool support and instead refer to a *separate project implementation plan* for these issues. This is handy if a RUP mentor does the main planning of the process and tool support, leaving the project manager to concentrate on all other issues and document them in the SDP. In our opinion, this method is preferred when planning larger implementations where development projects run in parallel.

A separate project implementation plan document may have an outline similar to an organizational implementation plan (as described in Chapter 6, "Planning the RUP Adoption"), but the detail level for the activities found in these plans would differ. Table 7.1 shows an extract of some process support activities for a sample project adopting parts of RUP's Requirements, Project Management, and Test disciplines and a tool for Configuration Management.

Activity	Kind of Support	Time	Participants
Project assessment	General	1st month	RUP mentor
RUP fundamentals	Process training	1st month	Everyone
Requirements management	Process training	2nd month	System analyst, requirements specifiers
Principles of software testing	Process training	3rd month	Test manager, test analysts, test designers
Clear case introduction	Tool training	2nd month	Configuration Management (CM) manager, selected developers
Use case model survey	Workshop	2nd month	System analyst, requirements specifier, one or more stakeholders, test manager, RUP mentor
Use case specifications	Workshop	2nd month	System analyst, requirements specifier; RUP mentor
Overall project planning (SDP, risk list)	Workshop	2nd month	Project manager, software architect, system analyst, test manager, RUP mentor
Iteration planning (inception)	Workshop	2nd month	Project manager, software architect, system analyst, test manager, RUP mentor
Test ideas	Workshop	3rd month	Test manager, test analysts, test designers, software architect, deployment manager, RUP mentor
Test cases, test data	Workshop	3rd month	Test manager, test analysts, test designers, RUP mentor
Clear case installation and setup	Tooling	2nd month	Clear case tool specialist, CM manager
Development case	General	2nd month, updated continuously	RUP mentor, process engineer (if different from RUP mentor)
Requirements artifacts	Artifact review: form, not content	3rd month	RUP mentor
Iteration assessment	Workshop	3rd month	Everyone
Lifecycle objective milestone (between the Inception and Elaboration phase)	Milestone review	3rd month	Project manager, software architect, system analyst, test manager, RUP mentor
...	...	...	...
Lifecycle architecture milestone (between the Elaboration and Construction phase)	Milestone review	5th month	Project manager, software architect, system analyst, test manager, RUP mentor
...	...	...	...

Table 7.1   *A Sample Activity List for a Project Implementation Plan*

7.4.1   Stand By for Changes

You should be prepared for changes. If the project changes, the RUP adoption may need to change as well. But beware of the first-level reaction of throwing away RUP as soon as your projects start running out of time. Is it likely that you made all the right decisions at the beginning of the implementation effort? Is it likely that you had all the information needed and that the information you had was correct? Is it likely that nothing around you will change during the implementation? No. No plan is sacred. A plan that has not been changed recently is probably incorrect.

Use the evaluations at the end of each iteration in the development projects as the main source of information that might cause you to adjust the implementation goals and the implementation plans. Also look for new opportunities that arise within the organization; it may be wise to adjust the original implementation plan in order to take advantage of such situations as the presence of a newly hired RUP expert, the purchase of new kinds of tools, and so on.

7.5   Communicating with People in the Organization

Do not forget to execute your communication plan (see "Developing a Communication Plan" in Chapter 6). People in the organization want to know how the implementation is proceeding and whether it is successful. Distribution of information about the decisions regarding the implementation and its progress needs to be handled in a structured manner. The receivers of the information can be divided into three groups:

1. Project team members who are using or are about to use RUP as their development process
2. Developers who have not been involved in the new process yet
3. Other people (nondevelopers) in the organization who won't perform any work in the process but will be affected indirectly by the changes (e.g., managers, purchasers, steering committee members, and so on)

These three groups need information of different kinds. For example, the project team members using RUP need detailed information about the configuration, but the nondevelopers need information about the changes in the results that will be presented to them. One of the most important pieces of information to communicate is the actual *purpose* and the *goals* of the implementation.

The organization can prepare the *information packages* needed and also perform *marketing work* within the organization. If an implementation takes place without an implementation project, there is a risk that very little information will spread outside the actual development project. Make sure to plan for communication and update the plan as needed after each implementation step.

Everyone in *the supported projects* should know what is happening on "the RUP front." Because your organization won't adopt all of RUP at once, there will still be people in your project *working the old way*. Even so, these people will likely be affected by the RUP adoption. Maybe they will get a new kind of document as input, or maybe they will hear people using a new language during coffee breaks. The least you should do is to inform them about the RUP adoption at information meetings, perhaps one to two times a month. That may be combined with some kind of written information, for instance, an e-mail newsletter (see Figure 7.2). If there is a project Web site, this is a good place for information as well.

7.6 Building Competence Among the Employees

When planning for a change, it is important to plan the individual development of the employees as well. One part of that development is training.

7.6.1 Training Sessions

Generally employees should receive training as close to the actual need as possible (just-in-time training). It might seem more cost-effective to have a massive training effort in the beginning of the implementation, but if people will not have a chance to practice their new skills soon, they will forget them.

In order to define what training is needed for each employee and when, *training paths* can be created for each role active in software development. For example, developers need an overview of RUP; knowledge

Hi, Project LS,

Some time has passed since the last newsletter, and we would like to inform you about what is happening with the adoption of RUP at LS. As you remember, we made an assessment of the current situation in February. We are still working with the same prioritized areas revealed in this assessment:

- CM (Configuration Management)
- Requirements Management
- Project Management
- Test

(Just to clarify, we will not introduce any changes in how design and coding are done at the moment. Please be aware, though, that the project plans and requirements specification will look different from what you are used to today.)

Furthermore, we have decided to use Release 2.0 as our target project for the adoption of RUP. Please note, though, that the CM from RUP and a CM tool will be introduced throughout LS, i.e., on Release 1.x as well.

According to RUP, the process to be used in a project should be documented in something called Development Case, and this has been put on the LS Server in a folder called "RUP at LS."

Next to come for Release 2.0:

1. "Process Review" of the Use Case Model consisting of a Use Case Model Survey and two Use Case Specifications at the moment.
   ("Process Review" = Richard and myself will give feedback on the form, not the content. We ensure that your model confirms with the guidance in RUP.)
2. "Process Review" of the Supplementary Specification.
3. "Process Review" of the Glossary.
4. Support during project planning.
5. Support that "Domain Reviews" are planned. (Only you who know your domain can make an agreement with the sponsor that everything documented is relevant and correct in terms of content.)
6. We will facilitate Part 2 of the Project Planning Workshop (May 15th) that Peter invited you to attend.
7. We will plan for test workshops.

What has been done for Release 2.0 so far?

- One 4-hour Use Case Model Survey workshop has been run.
- One 4-hour Use Case Model Specifications workshop has been run.
- One meeting with the sponsor regarding the adoption of RUP was held.
- One 4-hour Project Planning workshop has been run.

We (the members of the adoption project team) have also done some work "on our own." All documentation from this has been stored on the LS Server:

- A Development Organization Assessment (Project Assessment) has been documented and stored on the server.
- A Development Case has been written and stored on the server.

Regards,

Lotta and Richard (with Peter's approval)

Figure 7.2   *A sample e-mail newsletter*

about UML, analysis, and design; and an orientation about testing. The organization can help suggest suitable training for the different individuals as well as deliver some of the training.

7.6.2 Workshops

As a complement to regular training sessions, you can use *start-up workshops,* which you can also call *training workshops* or *work meetings.* In these workshops, the project group members work on their actual case and produce artifacts necessary for the project. Members from the implementation team lead the workshops. The idea here is that experienced workshop leaders lead the project group through the work the first time and transfer knowledge while necessary work is performed. The workshops can be regarded as "mini-courses" or refreshers after regular training sessions.

Examples of areas where these kinds of workshops have been used successfully are use case modeling, analysis modeling, and test planning. Do not confuse these workshops with the workshops described in RUP that are part of the software development work, such as use case modeling workshops. Those RUP workshops are solely focused on producing software (or intermediate results). The start-up workshops have a secondary purpose: to educate the project members so they can perform this work without further training support in the future.

Some organizations never expect the software development project members to be self-reliant regarding all workshops. This will be the case when the organization has a support organization for methodology and processes (see "Perform Ongoing Process Improvements" in Chapter 1). If the strategy, however, is that the project members *should* learn to lead the workshops themselves, it is important to appoint a *receiver* of the knowledge of how to behave as a workshop facilitator.

It is management's task to monitor the performance of the development projects and look for signs that the work is coming to a halt. As mentioned earlier, it is crucial that the project teams that start to use RUP deliver their systems on time. The implementation team can help keep the projects up to speed by transfering knowledge during workshops and by mentoring, thus reducing the "nonproductive time" when building competence.

7.7   Performing Reviews

There are several reasons why the organization should support the development projects with *reviews*. One of them is that during the RUP adoption, the implementation team will gain more and more experience about how certain RUP material should look in the context of the specific adaptation of RUP used in your organization. Reviews are an excellent opportunity to share that experience with others. Below we discuss two types of reviews that are common in all development projects: artifact reviews and milestone reviews.

7.7.1   Artifact Reviews

One question is often asked (or at least ought to be) within a development project using RUP for the first time: "Does this artifact comply with our configuration (adaptation) of RUP (and RUP itself)?" In a larger implementation where more than one pilot project is run in parallel, there is a risk that several "subcultures" may appear in terms of how to document the development in artifacts. The implementation team can review the artifacts that the development project team produces to make sure that the documentation is complete and follows the common process. For example, if the way to write use cases in different projects does not deviate from the guidelines in RUP, it will be easier to perform reviews and to exchange people between projects.

The implementation team should not assess the product itself, for example, whether the architecture is good or not. However, the implementation team can assist in creating *a good description* of the product. Having a good description might reveal deficiencies (e.g., in the architecture) that otherwise might not have been seen.

7.7.2   Milestone Reviews

One of the most common mistakes made by a project team using RUP for the first time is to cheat on fulfilling milestone criteria. This often happens when the project members are under pressure. If the architecture is not stable, you can't move into the Construction phase; if you do, you lie to yourself and others and in fact misuse RUP. The implementation team can assess whether the criteria are fulfilled and also help in arguing with management and steering groups about the importance of keeping the milestone model intact. However, this requires the implementation team to have experts in the specific area to be reviewed (e.g., architecture), and this is not always the case.

7.8   Performing Mentoring

If staffed correctly, the implementation team has *experts in certain areas* who can mentor specific roles as well as the implementation team as such. The areas for which a specific project team needs support differ depending on the experience of the participants. One area that often requires extra support in a project using RUP is project management because the iterative part of project planning is new to many project managers. Other common areas where mentoring usually is a good investment are requirements, analysis and design, and architecture. It is a good practice to appoint special mentors to the areas that need the most support. It is also good to have a mentor who takes care of all general process matters and coordinates the other mentors to create consistency.

In Chapter 11, "A Guide to Successful Mentoring," we have described how to behave as a mentor more thoroughly.

7.8.1   Training the Mentors

An organization can often benefit from having external mentors present in the beginning of an implementation effort. One goal for the mentors should be to become *redundant;* that is, the receivers of the mentoring should become *self-sufficient.* However, in a large implementation it will not be economically possible to have a sufficient number of external mentors. The implementation team can take responsibility for finding *internal* candidates and training them to become mentors in the later stages of the implementation.

One way to coach future mentors is to use *external mentors at the start* of the implementation and staff the pilot project with the mentor candidates. The candidates focus on a RUP subset (i.e., discipline) of the process of which they have working knowledge and, in addition to performing tasks in the development project, they spend time with an external mentor to learn the mentoring profession. In later stages of the implementation, the candidates can take over the "per discipline" mentoring while an external mentor takes the role of coordinating the internal mentors. Eventually one or more of the internal mentors will be able to take over that role as well, eliminating the need for external mentors. Figure 7.3 summarizes this process.

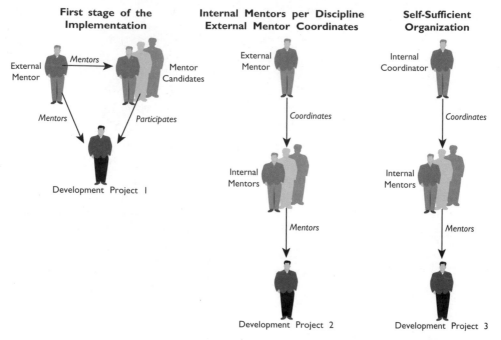

First stage of the Implementation

External Mentor — *Mentors* → Mentor Candidates

Mentors   *Participates*

Development Project 1

Internal Mentors per Discipline External Mentor Coordinates

External Mentor

Coordinates

Internal Mentors

Mentors

Development Project 2

Self-Sufficient Organization

Internal Coordinator

Coordinates

Internal Mentors

Mentors

Development Project 3

Figure 7.3   *An organization can afford only a limited number of external mentors. By using an external mentor to train internal mentors, there will be more RUP mentors available to support future projects in the organization.*

7.9   Conclusion

It is important to have external support for the development projects. Otherwise the adoption may slow down because it is hard to learn to use a new process without support and to develop quality software at the same time. RUP mentors who have experience both from applying RUP to different circumstances and from software development provide necessary support. Mentors help project members apply new knowledge to the project's particular problems. A typical support package consists of training to teach the theory, start-up workshops that bridge the gap between theory and practice, and other types of assistance, such as reviews.

In the next chapter, we will change perspective and focus on the project team receiving the support.

8

How to Adopt RUP in Your Project

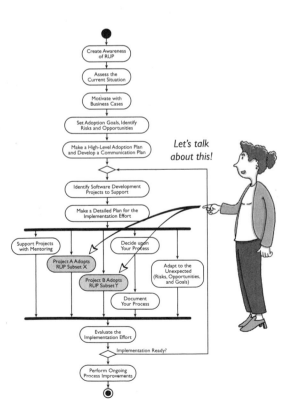

Let's talk about this!

Implementing RUP in a single software development project is *not* a minor task, even though it's less demanding than implementing RUP in an organization. Many factors impact the size of this task. One important factor is your current *process maturity*. Are the people who will staff your project used to working in a structured and predictable manner? Is it pretty clear what kind of documentation will be useful? How much of RUP do you plan to use? Actually, it is very important *not* to make the RUP adoption too big of a task! One of the secrets of a successful RUP implementation lies in the ability to decide upon a "just enough" amount (right-size) of RUP for your project to adopt without jeopardizing any of the objectives.

127

The main objective for every software development project—regardless of whether or not you're adopting RUP—should always be to successfully develop the intended software. Especially for that reason, it is important to *carefully plan* for your project's RUP adoption as well as *get support* for it so that it does well. Do not attempt too much, and make sure you benefit from what you do take on. Of course, your project's success is of interest to you and all the stakeholders, but it is also important for a potential rollout of RUP in your organization. (See the discussion of the sample goal "Ensure that every project that uses RUP succeeds" in the "Setting Adoption Goals" section in Chapter 6, "Planning the RUP Adoption.") To help you, find someone with experience, preferably a RUP mentor (also see Chapter 11, "A Guide to Successful Mentoring").

Perhaps your software development project is *part of an organizational initiative* of rolling out RUP across the organization. Perhaps your project is the pilot project. In any case, collaborating with the RUP implementation team is probably new to you. Just to set things straight here, your project manager is always in charge of your project's success in developing software. But because the real RUP adoption takes place on the project level, the success of the RUP implementation at the organization level therefore depends on your project. Ask for more help if you feel it's needed. Say no if you feel the implementation team pushes too many process demands on you. In this way you help your organization the most. And please be open minded and take some time to share your experiences of RUP, especially after the project has finished. The implementation team should help you with this (see Chapter 7, "Obtaining Support from the Organization").

So how do you adopt RUP within your project? In Figure 8.1 we present a simple flow of adoption activities that we recommend you perform. The subsequent sections in this chapter explore the details of the activities and guide you to further reading elsewhere in this book. The first thing your project team should do, preferably with some help, is to assess your project. Find out how you normally work and what your needs will be in this project. With that as input, you should select portions RUP to implement and plan how to achieve the required RUP knowledge. You do this in parallel with the ordinary project planning. After that, you run your project and get support on RUP. Finally, you share experiences with other people in your organization. This probably applies only if your project is part of an organizational RUP adoption.

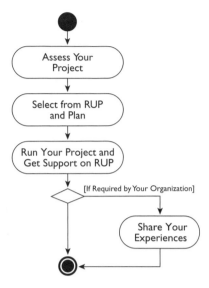

Figure 8.1   *A recommended flow of activities while adopting RUP in a single software development project*

8.1   Assessing Your Project

The project assessment forms the basis of your project's RUP adoption and enables you to "back the right horses" from the start. During the assessment, you look into the characteristics of your project and find out how the project members usually develop software. With that information at hand, the project manager can proceed with the next activity—planning the parts of RUP to introduce during the project.

If your project is part of an organizational RUP adoption, the implementation team should assist your project and provide assessors (RUP mentors) who make the project assessment for you.

8.1.1   Is RUP a Good Idea?

The first thing to figure out is whether RUP could apply at all to your project. (For simplicity, we'll talk about projects, but this information could apply to any software development assignment.) Answers to the following list of questions should provide you with the information you need to judge the applicability of RUP to a particular project.

1. Will the project develop software?
2. Will the project be staffed with people who have developed software before?
3. In general, are the project members interested in using RUP?
4. Does the project manager have a special interest in using RUP?

RUP includes guidance for software development. In order for your project to "match" and benefit from RUP, you should develop software of some kind.[1] That is not to say that the project has to involve completely new development starting from scratch! The project could just as well deal with *changing the configuration of a standard system* in order to match a certain need or problem. It could be evolution or *maintenance of existing software.* As long as the project has to do with finding a computerized solution to a set of functions defined as matching a certain need—for a business, for a market, or inside a technical system—RUP can be used.

Your project team should include people who have former software development experience. RUP won't teach you how to become a good programmer, for instance. RUP will guide you about *what* to do and even *how* to do many things, but basic software development knowledge is a prerequisite.

It is very hard to implement RUP within a team that is not at all interested in using RUP. Actually, we recommend that you do not use RUP if neither you nor the people who assist you can create any kind of interest.

It's very important to have a *project manager* who wants to use RUP. The project manager is in charge of all activities that take place in a project and makes them happen, including the RUP adoption. A RUP mentor only *supports* an adoption. The project manager has the most critical role during a RUP adoption. If the project manager doesn't want RUP, there will be no RUP.

---

1. Although RUP is intended for software development, many organizations get inspired by the concepts and ideas found in RUP and, for instance, use the terminology of artifacts, iterations, and the names of the phases for other areas as well. The use case modeling techniques described in RUP have been used for everything from laying out apple gardens to supervising a telecom network. Naturally, the amount of advice these applications get from RUP is very small. . . .

8.1.2   What Are the Characteristics of the Project?

The next thing to determine is what the project will do. Your project manager usually knows the answers to the questions listed below, but sometimes you'll need to consult the software architect.

1. What kind of system will you build (assemble, evolve, maintain)?
2. What will the technical platform be?
3. How big is the task? How difficult?
4. How long should it take?
5. How many people will be involved?

Read more about this in the "Types of Products and Projects" section in Chapter 4, "Assessing Your Organization."

8.1.3   How Do the Project Members Usually Develop Software?

The final thing to find out is how software is currently developed, including which aspects people think work well already and which don't, people's current knowledge, and their willingness to learn RUP. By asking the project members individually the following questions, you can survey the current process.

1. What are your roles? How do you normally work?
2. What documentation do you normally use? What documentation do you normally produce?
3. Which tools are used?
4. With whom do you normally communicate? Is it the same in this project?
5. How do you know what to do?
6. What is your view on how the overall development of software proceeds?
7. What do you know about RUP? What are your feelings about RUP in general?
8. What three things do you consider *good* about your work and this project? What three things do you consider *bad*?

Read more about this in the "What to Assess" section in Chapter 4, "Assessing Your Organization."

8.1.4   Documenting the Project Assessment

You should document your assessment findings in a bulleted list of the 15–20 topmost facts that summarize your project's situation (see Figure 8.2)

- *The team is new and on its way to establishing common routines.*

- *There is no collected set of requirements. Nonfunctional requirements are not documented.*

- *The test team asks for better specifications.*

- *A consultant who is good at RUP's Test discipline has been hired for the project.*

- *There is no change management of documents. Code is stored in tool X, documents on a common server and people's hard drives.*

- *The team will soon have a situation of more customers and several parallel installations.*

- *The project manager is responsible for requirements, project management, and delivery.*

- *The project develops Web applications with a lot of user interface requirements.*

- *There is a complex deployment environment whose setup is dependent on one individual.*

Figure 8.2   *Sample of project assessment findings*

and that might affect the RUP adoption in some way. Make sure everyone in the project agrees on that list.

If assessors from an organizational implementation team assist you, they should document their findings in a project assessment report. It's important that your project team agrees on that document and the summarized list of findings; ask for changes if you don't feel comfortable with these.

8.2   Selecting from RUP and Planning the Implementation

When your project's situation is known, you should choose a relevant subset from RUP for your project to adopt. Focus on areas where the need for a new process is substantial. You also need to plan for the process support required in order for the project members to learn and start working according to the selected parts of RUP. That support must be coordinated with other project activities; sometimes the scope of the RUP subset must be cut down because it becomes obvious that the project team hasn't got enough time to adopt it all. Pay attention to the tool support required by the chosen RUP subset. You probably need to plan for installation, configuration, and setup of a number of tools as well.

If your project is part of an organizational RUP adoption, the implementation team will provide RUP mentors to help you make a good selection from RUP as well as a list of recommended process support activities for you to put in your project plan.

8.2.1   Deciding upon and Documenting Your Process, Part 1

Depending upon what areas you consider to be weak, you choose applicable parts from RUP. Your project-specific process will be a mix of RUP and your old way of working. You should not take on too much RUP at once—you need to master the situation and not let the development be shaken to its foundations. At this stage (part 1) you make a rough selection most likely based on the disciplines[2] in RUP. You probably also cut out parts of each discipline you select to follow. Later (part 2) you will learn more details of your process selection (see "Running Your Project and Getting Support on RUP" later in this chapter). But disciplines are not at all the only way to express your process; read more in Chapter 9, "Deciding upon Your Process."

Many projects have big needs, and although the *main* recommendation is to adopt the selected parts of RUP rather deeply to become "a process in the heart of the employees," there are *some* cases where a wide and shallow strategy might be necessary; see Chapter 6, "Planning the RUP Adoption."

Your project-specific process, or at least the parts you select from RUP, should be documented in a *development case*. There are different ways to present the development case, including through the use of a normal document. Read more in Chapter 10, "Documenting Your Process." The development case not only documents your process but also should tell the readers which *tools* support which parts of your process.

---

2. The disciplines in RUP are Business Modeling, Requirements, Analysis & Design, Implementation, Test, Deployment, Configuration & Change Management, Project Management, and Environment.

8.2.2   Planning the Process Support

It is very hard to change a way of working if you don't get some *extra time* and some support in terms of training as well as practical assistance from someone with experience, preferably a RUP mentor. You ought to plan for process support on the parts from RUP selected for your project-specific process. Which RUP subsets require the most support, and how is that support best given? What training and mentoring is needed and when?

Training will most likely consist of a course in RUP basics for everyone as well as one or more in-depth courses for some project members. Mentoring can be provided individually to project members acting in certain RUP roles and sometimes to a group of people in a workshop (e.g., on how to perform use case modeling). RUP mentors can help people to get started with RUP and also to conduct reviews of documents, models, and project plans, ensuring that the guidance of RUP has been followed in a beneficial way in order for the project to reach its software development objectives.

If an organizational RUP implementation team assists your project, you should ask for *proactive support to be planned in advance* (to some extent). The initiatives for assistance should not come only from your project team calling in RUP mentors when you do not know what to do. Read more about this in Chapter 7, "Obtaining Support from the Organization." Figure 8.3 shows the RUP and tools adoption support given to a sample project adopting parts of RUP's Project Management, Requirements, and Test disciplines and a tool for Configuration Management. As you can see, the support is rather extensive in the beginning during the project's Inception and Elaboration phases.

8.2.3   Documenting the Process Support

Your project's process will be documented in a development case. But where should you document the activities for the process and tool support? Usually you document the process and tool support activities in the project's *normal project planning* only. If you use the Project Management discipline from RUP, the planning documents will consist of the software development plan (SDP) and a number of iteration plans. Among the other "normal" project activities, you will find RUP-related

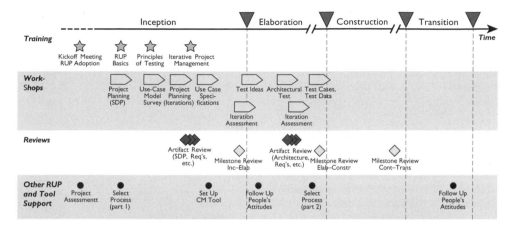

Figure 8.3   *Examples of the RUP adoption support given to a software development project*

activities—RUP training, RUP workshops, RUP reviews, and the RUP artifacts that are expected as deliverables. The SDP refers to the development case mentioned above.

If an organizational process team supports your project, the team may choose to document the process and tools support in a separate project implementation plan; see Chapter 7, "Obtaining Support from the Organization." No matter how the overview planning is documented, the activity list will look the same because all activities in a project should be included in an iteration plan.

8.3   Running Your Project and Getting Support on RUP

Your project is running and you start working according to the subset of RUP you have selected to be part of your project-specific process. A RUP mentor provides support on all RUP-related activities along the way. This support should be both proactive and reactive. *Proactive support* is the kind of support you can plan for in advance (see Figure 8.3 above); it consists of training, workshops, and reviews.

But because it is impossible to foresee the project team's needs completely, the RUP mentor also needs to give *reactive support* either individually to project members acting in certain RUP roles or sometimes to a group of people by conducting an extra workshop. Make sure you get enough support! A RUP mentor should be able to support the project manager by defining all the RUP-related detailed activities in the project's iteration plans (see below).

Another thing that is impossible to foresee is the final process your project will use. You have made a first selection from RUP, but you need to find out how that selection will look when applied to your case when the project is running. Probably several situations will appear and raise questions: "How shall we do this?" "What would this be for us?" A RUP mentor should help you fine-tune your process and really listen to you and your project members to make the process fit your needs.

If an organizational implementation team supports your project's RUP adoption, this team will provide you with RUP mentors. Read more about the support to expect in Chapter 7, "Obtaining Support from the Organization." In Chapter 11, "A Guide to Successful Mentoring," you can learn why RUP mentors are important and how they should work and behave.

8.3.1 Getting Support Down to the Activity Lists in the Project's Iteration Plans

It is important to receive *concrete* support from your RUP mentor. Figure 8.4 shows an iteration plan for the only iteration in the Inception phase for the sample project mentioned earlier (a project that adopts parts of RUP's Requirements, Project Management, and Test disciplines and a tool for Configuration Management).

8.3.2 Deciding upon and Documenting Your Process, Part 2

You will work out the final project-specific process while running the project. Your project's way of using RUP will be decided upon and documented in one way or another. As mentioned earlier, at the start of the project you will have a rough selection (ideas or drafts) of what your process will be (part 1 of process tailoring). When exposed to the specific problems of your project, you will refine and detail that first selection to

1. **Introduction**

   1.1 Purpose

   To describe what will happen short-term in the project. There will be one iteration plan for each planned iteration (see Ref 1, SDP). The project manager uses the iteration plan to plan all detailed activities and follow them up. The project members use the iteration plan to see what they are expected to do in the project and which other activities they might depend on.

   1.2 Scope

   The first iteration in Inception (hopefully the only one!).

   1.3 References

   Ref 1   SDP (Software Development Plan)

   Ref 2   Risk List

   Ref 3   Use Case Model Survey

   1.4 Overview

   At first the objectives of the iteration are described as a list of artifacts and to what extent these should be ready (expressed in %). The risks addressed and use cases realized during the iteration are listed. The resources working are listed by name, role, and level of involvement (expressed in %). At the end you will find a complete activity list, a "to do" list including activity, who the activity is assigned to, when it is expected to be ready, and a reference to the corresponding RUP activity (if any).

2. **Iteration Objectives (Evaluation Criteria)**

   To roughly define the requirements and to suggest ideas for a solution, a "paper-only" architecture. To conclude Inception. The iteration will end June 13, 2003.

   The following artifacts will be produced/worked on during the iteration:

   – Use Case Model

   – Use Case Model Survey (~80% ready)

   – Use Case Specifications for prioritized use cases (~20% ready in total)

   – Supplementary Specification (~80% ready)

   – Glossary (~90% ready)

   – Paper-only architecture (~100% ready)

   – SDP (~80% ready)

   – Iteration Plan for e1 (first iteration in Elaboration) (~80% ready)

   – CM Plan (~40% ready)

   – Master Test Plan (~10% ready)

3. **Risks**

   #5, Not enough resources (see Ref 2).

4. **Use Cases**

   Not applicable in Inception.

5. **Resources**

Name	Role	Working x-%
Peter	Project manager	90%
Sandra	Software architect	60%
Sid	System analyst, requirements speicifer	90%
Rebecca	Requirments specifier	90%
Timothy	Test manager	10%
Lotta	RUP mentor	20%

(Continues)

Figure 8.4   *Extracts of an iteration plan during the Inception phase*

---

6. Activity List

#	Activity	Resp.	Start	End	Comment ▭= RUP activity
1	Workshop, Use Case Model Survey	Lotta	3 Jan.	3 Jan.	Participants: Everyone ▭ *Find Actors and Use Cases* ▭ *Structure the Use Case Model*
2	Write Use Case Model Survey	Sid	4 Jan.	11 Jan.	▭ *Find Actors and Use Cases*
3	Write Supplementary	Rebecca	6 Jan.	15 Jan.	▭ *Detail the Software Requirement*
4	Write Glossary	Sid	4 Jan.		▭ *Capture a Common Vocabulary*
5	Write Use Case Specifications for "Register new member"	Sid	7 Jan.		▭ *Detail the Use Case*
6	Workshop Project Planning SDP, 1st	Lotta, Peter	10 Jan.		▭ *Plan Phases and Iterations*
7	Workshops Project Planning SDP, 2nd	Lotta, Peter	11 Jan.		▭ *Plan Phases and Iterations* ▭ *Identify and Assess Risk* ▭ *Prioritize Use Cases* ▭ *Develop Iteration Plan*

Figure 8.4   *Extracts of an iteration plan during the Inception phase (continued)*

---

make up your final process (part 2 of process tailoring). Any need to customize the process (extend it or change it slightly) should be taken care of as soon as possible in order for you to create an effective process. A RUP mentor should be able to help you. But remember that the main purpose of the project is to deliver software; the delivery must never be postponed by any long-lasting process documentation activities. The decisions about how to do things should be documented "quick and dirty" (but still documented!). Later this quick-and-dirty documentation may evolve to proper guidelines, checklists, templates, and so on.

If your project is part of an organizational RUP adoption, you know your project's application of RUP will be of much interest to other people within your organization. If you have RUP mentors from an implementation team supporting you, they will help you with the application of RUP and your needs for tailoring/customization (if any). The RUP mentors should write down what have proven to be good ways to work in your project and then find ways to merge and insert these techniques into existing RUP activities. In this way the RUP mentors prepare for the harvesting and collection of working processes from the projects (see the next section).

Read more about tailoring/customization of RUP in Chapter 9, "Deciding upon Your Process." An easy way to document a project's application of RUP is to write guideline documents, but there are other ways too; read more in Chapter 10, "Documenting Your Process."

8.4 Sharing Your Experiences

Your experiences of RUP during your project can be helpful and interesting to others within your organization, especially if you are part of an organizational RUP adoption. Perhaps your project marks the first time RUP has been applied within your organization. You should spend some time sharing your experiences. You could do this in various ways: *talk informally* to other people about what you have done, how you liked it, and so on; *write something down,* hopefully in the form of a success story; or run a meeting with the goal of telling your story.

If your project is part of an organizational RUP adoption, the implementation team will *arrange opportunities* for you to share your thoughts. You could share your experiences in person formally by talking at RUP experience meetings or seminars or just informally by talking to another person who will take on the same RUP role in another project. You could share your experiences in written format via your organization's RUP Web site; see Chapter 10, "Documenting Your Process." If it hasn't already done so, the implementation team will *harvest* your project to find valuable material in the form of guidelines, checklists, templates, details, and customizations of various RUP activities; examples of RUP artifacts; and so on. These will be *merged* with your organization's process on the RUP Web site and shared with all people in your organization. Upcoming project teams will benefit a lot from examining what other project teams have done and reusing successful parts of the process, which will also speed up their usage of RUP.

Your project has applied and tried out the process. Delivering the project on time is often a good-enough result. However, if the RUP implementation team has chosen a more formal way to follow up the project's performance, this is the time to collect measurements and try to discover whether the results of the project are aligned with the organizational RUP adoption goals. Read more in Chapter 5, "Motivating the RUP Adoption."

This is also a good time to follow up people's attitudes regarding the changes in ways of working.

8.5   What Will Happen after the Project?

The project is over, and hopefully some parts of RUP were successfully adopted. You may wonder whether there will be any further benefits from RUP. In fact, we have some very good news. *You will benefit a lot from the RUP adoption during the maintenance of your software!*

How you will benefit depends of what parts of RUP you adopted. If you adopted use case modeling for the requirements, it will be much easier for new people to maintain the developed software and understand it. If you adopted complete model-driven development (use case model, design model, code generation), you can quickly and safely make functional changes to the software. If you adopted the Test discipline, you have documented test cases that will help you make sure the software still works after a change. Not to mention what a good architecture can do for a software system that will last and evolve for years!

8.6   Conclusion

It all happens in the projects! A project's adoption of RUP will differ depending on whether it is supported by the organization or is doing the adoption by itself. However, the same types of activities apply, namely, assessing the project, selecting a subset from RUP, and planning activities regarding the adoption together with the normal development activities. Hopefully the project team can get support from a mentor while the project is running. After the project ends, experiences regarding the process should be shared. This is especially important if the project is part of an organizational adoption of RUP. Knowledge about RUP and software development should be transferred from project to project.

In the next chapter, we will guide you in how to decide on elements of your process.

9

Deciding upon Your Process

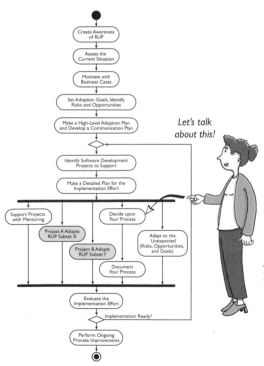

Let's talk about this!

Every organization is unique and has different demands regarding what constitutes a suitable software development process. Of course, all software development projects running within the organization will not need exactly the same process, but they will likely share many parts. During the project teams' adoption of RUP, they will adapt RUP to their needs. Their experiences[1] of RUP—perhaps in conjunction with other established processes at your organization—are valuable. They enlighten the understanding of what is a suitable software development process

---

1. Experiences may typically appear as additional guideline documents, sample artifacts, extra activities and tasks, or just thoughts about what parts of RUP were particularly useful.

at your organization. The projects enable you to decide what parts of RUP to implement on the organization level.

This chapter covers how to decide what process to use, whereas Chapter 10, "Documenting Your Process," covers how you may *document* these decisions.

When deciding upon (or growing or fine-tuning) an organizational process,[2] the RUP process framework should be the basis and the starting point. You will select parts of RUP to focus on, you will add needed process information not present in RUP, and occasionally you will change RUP slightly to fulfill your needs. The idea is that development project team members "depart" from this organization-level process platform when defining their project-level process (and/or development case), but that they also "arrive" there in order to "deliver" their experiences and share them with future project members, who then have better support than they would get from RUP alone.

Many organizations choose to name their process (see Figure 9.1). This is a good idea because the organization's process framework would not, and should not, be equal to RUP after a while. It won't include all parts of RUP, and it will include things not in RUP. Instead of saying "our RUP configuration," you may give your baby a name! It's much more pleasant, and it's also practical to have a common name for it. Also, we have noticed that naming the configuration creates ownership and liability and therefore facilitates the change.

The assessment results in recommendations of what parts of RUP to implement. These recommendations are normally not that detailed, and you need to spend some time selecting parts of RUP to use. More often than not, you also need to add other process material.[3] This preparation should not be too extensive before trying your process on actual software development projects. As a rule of thumb, spend no more than one to three weeks in preparation. We have seen organizations spend months on process configuration; they come up with very nice Web sites, but the fact

---

2. Other names we might use for *organizational process* are *organization-level process, organization's development process, your process, your adaptation,* and *your RUP configuration.*
3. A guideline document or document template is the simplest form of process material.

Figure 9.1 *Giving your organizational process a name creates ownership and will be beneficial and supportive for the change in general.*

is that nothing was implemented in real projects and no one used the process configuration, not even one or two years after its completion. Through the projects actually using RUP, you finally learn what parts of RUP to select and include in your process. It is in the software development projects that you actually decide upon your process.

But what if the development projects at your organization are very different from each other? What if there is no single process that fits them all?

Actually, this is exactly the case! There won't be one process that fits all your projects. Small projects are very different from large projects. New development projects are very different from maintenance projects. Depending on the technology platform used, projects differ a lot. Therefore, your organizational process typically should contain a number of "standard RUP configurations" for your project teams to select among and use as a starting point.

In a way, an organizational process (process *framework*[4]) can be explained as the sum (not the intersection!) of all the development cases of all its projects. This means that *your* process, just like RUP, will have some degrees of freedom. The goal when building your process is not to figure out one single "process thread" through RUP that all your projects must follow. A better goal is that your process should support in a useful way all different kinds of projects that take place in your organization. You should add the experiences gained from former projects so that new project teams can learn and start with much better support than the first ones had. (Read more below in "Adding Process Information.")

Remember that projects are always different. Sometimes we think that organizations overinflate the importance of working in a common and controlled way, at least when they come up with rather extensive lists of RUP artifacts that they state are mandatory for *every* project. This is a common beginner's mistake. First, there is no "one size fits all" solution, and second, if people think of processes as being just heavy documents to fill in, their expectations seem to come true. To succeed with a process implementation, we need to look beyond the artifacts.

9.1   Selecting Parts of RUP

"Select? We don't want to select, we want to use all of RUP!" "We have chosen RUP because it is a configurable process. We will use only X, Y, and Z from RUP." It doesn't matter what your starting point is—*everyone* has to start by selectively using parts of RUP. Even if your goal is to use all[5] of RUP,

---

4. RUP is really not a process but rather a process framework. The specific instance each project uses is a process. A development case then describes a process.
5. Actually, if your goal is to *definitely* use all of RUP, you will fail. RUP is too large for any single project to use it all.

you are likely to fail if you do not implement RUP incrementally. You need to select subsets of RUP to implement in one step after another en route to getting "the full RUP" (or rather, "your ultimate process," if you like).

Which parts should you select? How should you select them? When should you select what? There are different ways to start the adaptation. There are also different ways to define it. As discussed in Chapter 4, "Assessing Your Organization," the basic idea is to first address the areas where you have the biggest problems due to a lack of good work processes (the areas where you feel the most "pain.") But what if you feel pain all over? What if everything is chaotic and ad hoc? In that situation, we recommend the following initial steps for most organizations.

1. Define requirements with use cases.
2. Use the four phases of RUP, including milestones and the architecture-first approach.
3. Run test cases derived from use cases.
4. Develop iteratively.

But isn't iterative development the most important thing with RUP? Yes, of course it is! But that does not mean it has to be the first thing to select for your implementation. It may be too risky—transitioning to iterative development is one of the most difficult things for organizations to achieve, and it tends to be a rather large change. The approach of taking on the biggest risk first may suit software development but *not* process implementation. Remember that people who are happy and continuously improving their RUP skills form the key for success of a RUP implementation. The approach of addressing the biggest *pain* first applies better to process implementation, and, believe us, more people (and projects!) suffer from bad requirements specifications than from a lack of iterative development.[6]

In our experiences, everyone just loves to learn use cases. And because more or less every company can improve the requirements area, selecting use cases for your first RUP subset is seldom a bad idea. By defining

---

6. Which parts of RUP do you *gain most* from implementing—always the parts where you have the biggest problems? Not necessarily. It is also important to consider the lifetime of the system being built. If you know in advance that your system won't last for very long, it is not advisable to spend too much time on architecture work. Thus, if you're in this situation, do not implement or perform RUP's architecture activities (found in the Analysis & Design and Implementation disciplines).

use cases, you get nice secondary effects. Everyone can read them and get a good understanding of the proposed system. With all needed functionality described in flows, the programmers get inspired to find nice solutions but are still kept aware of the main purpose of the system. The acquirer (orderer) and users of the system get involved in shaping the system early. The testers benefit from having use cases as input when defining test cases.

But let us stop praising use cases now and dig into the techniques of selecting RUP elements. How should you select from RUP? What things can you select? A common view is that first you select a discipline and then you select some artifacts. That's not wrong, but let us explore the whole spectrum of what can be used as a base (quantity) when selecting from RUP.

9.1.1   Disciplines

Probably the first thing to address when building your process is which disciplines in RUP you should use. This is because the nine disciplines in RUP are very visible. Selecting the disciplines first has some advantages.

+   There are only nine things to select from, which makes it easy for the creator of the process.
+   The removal of a whole discipline not to be covered is easy to understand for the users of the process.

Unfortunately, there is one major drawback.

−   The content of a whole discipline may be too big to grasp in one increment (and maybe you will not need everything anyway).

We have found that starting with the disciplines works fine during the early high-level discussions regarding what areas to focus on. In these meetings, managers make such decisions as, "We will focus on the Requirements and Test disciplines at the beginning," "We will skip the Business Modeling discipline entirely," and "We'll continue handling the Deployment discipline as we do today."

But once you've started the real RUP adoption, that is, in a software development project, you will soon find that the entire discipline (such as

Requirements) is very big. You'll need more guidance on exactly what to use *within* the discipline.

9.1.2 Artifacts

Configuring with artifacts as a base is probably the easiest thing to do. If you were to ask the people who created RUP and consult the metamodel that lies behind it all, you would find that a configuration nearly always starts by selecting artifacts. First you select the RUP artifacts you will need in order to develop software, which in turn leads to the corresponding activities and roles. (Remember that for every artifact in RUP there is one responsible RUP role, and from every artifact you can trace to the RUP activities that produce the artifact.)

Choosing the artifacts first has one main advantage.

+ This way you can make the process very small and precise, which may be good for its users.

But there are also disadvantages.

− The process creator has to look into many artifacts, and the users' exact needs are hard to predict.
− The process description becomes a table of artifacts that users usually do not find attractive to read. (With the focus on artifacts, users tend to look at their work as "what artifacts to produce" instead of "what tasks to perform."[7])

Too much focus on whether you need this or that artifact isn't good, especially not on the organizational level. On the project level, however, you will have figured out exactly what artifacts are needed and should be produced . . . by the end of the development project! In other words, it's very hard to predict a project's exact need for artifacts. The size of the project, whether the project team is geographically widespread or not, and the complexity of the system being built (among other things) impact the number of artifacts needed. Always remember that the most important task of a software development project is to produce code and build the

---

7. You may choose to *document* your configuration in another way, perhaps showing the activities that create the selected artifacts, which is less of a disadvantage.

system. Expensive production of in-between artifacts should be kept to a minimum. Do not hinder this by requiring lots of mandatory artifacts on the organizational level.

But don't think that all in-between artifacts can be skipped! The artifacts that we favor more that others are the *model* artifacts: the use case model, the design model, and so on. RUP *is* model-driven development, and it's the various UML models that take you from ideas to a valid system. Other favorites are the key artifacts of controlled iterative development: the risk list, the project plan, and the iteration plan.

If artifacts form the basis for configuration, sometimes project members who are new to RUP do not understand exactly what they need to produce at what time. Then it is a good idea to complement the list of artifacts and the templates from RUP with examples of completed artifacts relevant for the specific project (i.e., examples from the business in which your organization engages).

9.1.3   Activities

The work performed to create an artifact is sometimes more important than the final artifact itself. For instance, having an excellent vision of the software to be produced is far more important than the actual document describing the vision. There are many reasons why basing a configuration on activities is a good approach.

+   The focus on activities feels natural and makes the process easy to use. (You can look up the activities in RUP and follow their step-by-step descriptions.)
+   The iteration plans contains activities to perform, which creates a nice project–process connection for the users.

But there is also a disadvantage.

−   It may be hard to make sure that the process will work between disciplines. (This is an issue for the process creator: What must one person produce in order for the next person to perform his or her work well?)

By putting activities in focus, instead of artifacts (documents), it is easier to stay in line with the spirit of RUP (see Chapter 3, "What Is a RUP Project?"). Your goal should be to produce working software using as few artifacts as possible. But even though some artifacts are handled very informally or even skipped, you cannot skip the activities in the same way. Most activities in RUP still need to be performed in order to produce software of good quality.

9.1.4   Tools

Sometimes the process adaptation may begin with a tool (e.g., a change management tool). This can be the case if the organization has purchased a tool to solve a specific problem and it becomes clear that the process needs to be changed in order to use the tool to its full potential. Then all activities involving the tool are selected to build up the process. This has some advantages.

+   The process aligns with effective tool support.
+   The tool helps the organization implement the process.

But there will be problems if either of the following situations occurs.

−   The tool does not align with RUP.
−   The tool does not address any of the identified problem areas or solves only a few of them.

Generally speaking, when implementing a process, it is important to have the appropriate tools. We do not want to introduce tedious manual tasks because that gives people bad feelings about RUP. For example, asking people to draw all the UML symbols from scratch in a tool whose main purpose is to create presentations is not a good idea.

But tools can also help in another way. Because tools have rather concrete and predetermined functions, the implementation of a new tool is sometimes easier to handle than the implementation of a new set of activities. You can hide the process implementation behind a tool, which forces people to work in a new and better way.

9.1.5   Best Practices

The best practices[8] on which RUP is based lead to process "chunks" that have many similarities with the disciplines. For example, develop

---

8. The six best practices valid in the software industry and on which RUP is based are (1) develop iteratively, (2) manage requirements, (3) model visually (UML), (4) use component architectures, (5) continuously verify quality, and (6) manage change.

iteratively ↔ the Project Management discipline; manage require-ments ↔ the Requirements discipline; and continuously verify quality ↔ the Test discipline.

But the recommendation to model visually covers more than one disci-pline because visual modeling takes place in the three disciplines (Requirements, Analysis & Design, and Implementation), so *using the model visually best practice* as the basis for configuration has the following advantages.

+   You can unambiguously express or formulate a key process subset of three core disciplines.
+   You can put the focus on tool artifacts only (which are models in a modeling tool, in this case, of the model visually best practice) rather than documents.

But in general there are drawbacks to basing a configuration on best practices.

−   The process content required to cover a whole best practice might be too big for the users to grasp.
−   Dependencies between different best practices might cause problems when using one best practice and omitting another. (For example, continuous quality verification is very dependent on iterative devel-opment. You cannot implement the first best practice fully until the other one is implemented as well.)

As a matter of curiosity: We know of an organization that used best practices in a special way for its RUP implementation. Many project teams wanted to adopt RUP at the same time, and there were not enough mentors to support them. (Read about the importance of men-toring in Chapter 11, "A Guide to Successful Mentoring"). The project teams were encouraged to implement best practices but were asked to avoid calling this a RUP approach because in a previous attempt to adopt RUP many projects had failed in their RUP implementations due to lack of experienced support. Best practices are not RUP specific at all, and although RUP incorporates them, you can adopt one or more best practices without adopting RUP. (If the team fails due to lack of support, at least RUP and the official implementation effort cannot be blamed.)

9.1.6   Going beyond the RUP Base: RUP Plug-Ins

So far we have more or less assumed that you will make your selection from the RUP base, that is, the classic, standard content of the default RUP Web site. But you should also look into the extensive list of available RUP plug-ins because one or more of them may have content that suits your circumstances. You can find RUP plug-ins developed by IBM Rational Software as well as many other companies, either for free or for a cost.[9]

The name *plug-in* reveals the technique used to include the extra process content. In the RUP Builder tool (see below) you load/unload plug-ins and generate a new process Web site, which includes the process content of your loaded plug-ins merged with the RUP base content in a way determined by the creators of the plug-ins. Read more in Chapter 10, "Documenting Your Process," if you want to create a RUP plug-in to include your own extensions.

The content of a RUP plug-in may vary widely. Tool vendors typically add guidelines on how to use their tools and techniques and connect these guidelines to one or more activities in RUP. Others provide RUP plug-ins that define some extra roles, activities, and artifacts (including descriptions and guidelines), all addressing a rather cohesive process area to extend—or to replace—the RUP base, for instance, to add support for developing real-time applications and applications with extensive human interactions. First you need to decide what plug-ins to use. As a second step, you may need to select subsets (e.g., disciplines, artifacts, activities, and so on) from within the RUP plug-ins, similar to selecting subsets from the RUP base.

9.1.7   How RUP Builder Can Help You Select a Subset

In the RUP Builder tool, you can select and deselect the content of your RUP Web site. This way you can generate your own process Web site whenever you want the content to differ from the RUP base. But within RUP Builder there are also ways to help you select an appropriate subset from RUP.

Small, Medium, and Large Subsets We often hear people say that RUP is overwhelming and that it is hard to know where to start when selecting a subset to work with. To help address this difficulty, RUP Builder provides

---

9. RUP plug-ins may be downloaded from the RUP Resource Center (http://www.rational.net/rupexchange).

three different preconfigured subsets of RUP based on project size: Small, Medium, and Large (Classic). Selecting Small or Medium speeds up the configuration process because you can choose among fewer items—or you can use these subsets as they are. Nonetheless, it is common to start from the Classic subset to avoid overlooking specific parts of the process that may be important for a particular project.

RUP Plug-Ins Regardless of which starting point you choose, you might want to look for additional process information in the form of RUP plug-ins. By using RUP Builder to select your starting point (see above) and to browse the plug-ins to load/unload, you can get a process framework that fits your needs reasonably well. After that, selecting your configuration is easier.

Process Components The entire RUP content is divided into nine disciplines, and each discipline is divided into a number of *process components*. Each process component basically contains a number of roles, activities, and artifacts. These process components become visible within RUP Builder. The division into process components was inspired by the solution component model (see the next section) but with a stronger attempt to create components with very few dependencies on other components.

Configuring with process components has the following advantages.

+   It offers support for generating a RUP Web site with exactly the content you have decided to use.
+   It allows a more granular selection than disciplines, which is better for the user of the process.
+   It provides a less granular selection than artifacts, which is better for the creator for the process.

Of course, this approach also has disadvantages.

−   It can be hard to see the correlation between a process component and a particular development problem being solved.
−   The process component does not include tools.

If you generate your own RUP Web site using RUP Builder, you will encounter process components, within the RUP base and possibly within the RUP plug-ins you consider including. Be careful, however, when excluding/replacing the RUP base content. Many people will feel "uncertain" when RUP looks different from the original RUP and will question what has been removed. Even if another process, for example, instead of the Test discipline, is used within the organization, there will still be details of RUP's Test discipline that people find valuable and want to access. Making use of the process views (see Chapter 10, "Documenting Your Process"), which you also configure and set up in RUP Builder, might be a better alternative.

9.1.8   Other Ways to Get Help for the Selection Process

It is not a trivial task to find a suitable process, nor is it trivial to define the process subsets to implement in each step of a step-by-step adoption of RUP. So how can you get help? The best thing is to talk to someone who has already applied RUP in a similar situation. If you can't find such a person within your organization, you will need to find someone external. Read more in How Can a Mentor Help You Decide upon Your Process? later in this chapter.

Apart from human help, we have already mentioned the preconfiguration concept of the Small, Medium, and Large subsets and process components found in RUP Builder. In RUP and in PEP,[10] you will find additional guidance on, as RUP calls them, "process discriminants" when determining the right process during a particular circumstance. We also know of some research conducted in the area of simplifying process selection, based on the idea that given a certain project characteristic—for example, the use of a legacy system—it should be possible to define a process subset that matches that characteristic [Karlsson 2002].

We have good experiences ourselves with a preconfiguration concept known as the *solution component model*, which you can read about next. Solution components have similarities with process components but stress the fact that each component solves a particular software development problem that an organization might have.

---

10. PEP refers to Process Engineering Process, a RUP adoption process. See the Preface of this book or the RUP Resource Center (http://www.rational.net/rupcenter) for more information.

Solution Components: An Idea for Simplifying Configuration   In this section we explain one way to simplify the task of making a good selection from RUP in order to improve your process. We present a kind of model for configuration—the solution component model—that our colleagues in Sweden and we have successfully used for some years.

A solution component within this model contains a not-too-big, not-too-small, cohesive *process subset* (activities, roles, and artifacts) as well as the appropriate *tool* supporting that process subset. Either you take a component as a whole or you leave it out completely. The components make the RUP configuration easy, and the stated relations between the components simplify the planning of a step-by-step RUP implementation. For instance, if you introduce the Test Management component during the first step of your RUP implementation, it is easier to introduce the related Test Automation component during the second step.

The roughly 20 components provide *solutions to problems*. The problems that may be solved are related to software development, such as creation of solutions for the wrong problem (through inadequate problem analysis and requirements gathering), late discovery of faults, poor quality, and so on. A full-fledged solution to such problems consists of both process and tool.

Configuring with solution components has the following advantages.

+   It offers a more granular selection than disciplines, which is better for the user of the process.
+   It offers a less granular selection than artifacts, which is better for the creator of the process.
+   Tools are selected in conjunction with the process parts.
+   In this problem-oriented approach, the selected configuration aims to solve problems (which is important when implementing RUP).

There is also a disadvantage.

−   This approach may not work if you use tools other than IBM Rational Software tools.

Here is a brief summary of how to use the solution component model during a RUP implementation.

First there is the *configuration*. During the assessment (see Chapter 4, "Assessing Your Organization"), we look for software development–related problems within an organization. An example of such a problem is inaccurate understanding of end user needs. A solution to this problem is provided within the Requirements with Use Cases solution component, which mainly contains the use case model, supplementary specification, and glossary artifacts, along with corresponding RUP activities, RUP roles, and an IBM Rational Software visual modeling tool.

But the problem is not solved until the organization really works according to the process subset and successfully uses the tool. This leads us to the *implementation aspect*. We need to train the organization to practice the process subset and use the supporting tool efficiently, making sure that the organization builds up necessary knowledge and skills. For each solution component, there is a recommended sequence of implementation support (e.g., training, workshops, role-based mentoring, follow-up reviews, and so on), which has been proven to result in a successful knowledge transfer.

In a step-by-step RUP implementation, these two aspects always go hand in hand. In each step, a configuration consisting of some new solution components is defined and implemented. The complete RUP configuration grows step by step, until the day that the organization achieves the ultimate (good-enough) process.

9.1.9 Things to Not Exclude

You have a lot of freedom when selecting parts of RUP to include in your process. As long as you select parts that will improve the current way of working, you will obtain benefits. However, there is one thing you must never cheat on: the milestone between the Elaboration and Construction phases or, to be more specific, the architecture-first approach (which basically means: do not start coding the detailed functionality until the overall technical solution has been chosen and proven to work).

We once heard of a project manager who insisted that on date D his project would enter the Construction phase. "No," the RUP mentor said, "you can't do that because you don't have a solution regarding the communication with the external system X, and you haven't tried out the in-house framework for Enterprise Java Beans that is supposed to be part of your solution." The project manager responded, "I must pass the milestone on that date because that is what is stated in the project plan, and I have promised the steering committee. . . ."

The milestones and phases are *not* time-boxed, meaning that even if there are target dates, phases will not end if the conditions for the milestone aren't fulfilled. Note that the milestones and phases are essential in RUP and should be included in your process as soon as possible. When is that? As soon as your organization is prepared to start using them correctly. (The project manager in the example above should have stayed with old names for phases or, even better, brought along someone involved in the RUP implementation to communicate and educate the steering committee on the changes involved with RUP.)

A general rule for a RUP implementation is that when you start using the names and wordings that RUP uses for various things, you must understand their meaning and use them correctly! For instance, never hide an old waterfall process behind a RUP façade, where old phase names have been replaced by new RUP phase names but no other changes have been made. And do not start to use the names of the RUP artifacts if they haven't been created by following the step-by-step descriptions and guidelines of the corresponding RUP activities. If you do that, you may undermine the RUP implementation or make it more difficult. Be fair; do not sail under false colors!

9.2   Adding Process Information

RUP gives you a starting point for developing software in general; then you expand on this to develop software in your organization in particular. This is done not only by selecting plug-ins but also by adding a lot of good advice that applies to your organization. You take RUP closer to your reality, step by step. And as the process support becomes more precise, it becomes more valuable and effective for you, and you will get better and better at developing software with RUP. Deciding upon your process continues as long as there are RUP projects running in the organization. You will extend the RUP knowledge base with organization-unique knowledge. Collecting various guidelines and documents from projects is one way this happens; more thoroughly refining and creating specialized RUP activities and RUP artifacts is another.

Not all additions to RUP that suit a specific project will be reusable by other projects in your organization, but many will be! New guidelines and artifacts may be easy to communicate within the organization. It will be harder to convey more complex process elements like activities, roles, and even disciplines. But there is help—the RUP tools enable you to create your own plug-ins to be reused by others in your organization. Read more about this in Chapter 10, "Documenting Your Process."

9.2.1   Adding Guidelines and Examples

Adding guidelines and examples created by a development project to your organizational process is easy because they are not vital parts of the process. People in your organization will feel a need for the information. Often the culture or software development style of an organization can be communicated through guidelines.

9.2.2   Adding Disciplines, Roles, Activities, and Artifacts

At times you will need to add new activities and artifacts to your selection of RUP. Maybe the domain you work within is very specific and parts of it are not covered by the RUP base or any of the available plug-ins. Or perhaps you found a new way to perform a certain part of software development that you want to try instead of using the methods prescribed by RUP. If you plan to add many activities, you might want to add a whole discipline.

Tools for proceeding with these kinds of additions are RUP Modeler, RUP Organizer, and RUP Builder (see Chapter 10, "Documenting Your Process"). These tools help you make sure that the additions will be reused consistently in your organization and will be easy to maintain between different releases of RUP.

9.2.3   Adding a Project Management Method

There may be processes and methods in the organization that need to be merged when adopting RUP. Many companies have an established project management method. This method typically consists of a number of mandatory project documents as well as guidelines on how these documents shall be handled. Often the same project management method is used for both software and nonsoftware projects.

It is very common to merge an existing project management method with activities and artifacts within the RUP Project Management discipline. Usually such a merge starts by adding the iteration plan and iteration assessment artifacts to the current project management method. Sometimes there is a risk document already within the method; otherwise, the RUP risk list artifact is added.

Steps, stages, progress indicators, tollgates, and decision points used in the existing project management method are compared with the phases and milestones of RUP. Probably some mapping is possible, but sometimes the ambition to create uniformity is foolish. What makes a good and constructive milestone depends on what the project does. If the project builds software, a milestone indicating the point in time when the key solution has been tried in code has proven to be smart and beneficial. But if the project builds something that has high material costs (e.g., a bridge), such a "cut the first sod" milestone is very expensive. Because the move from drawings to a complete bridge is fairly predictable, a "drawings ready" milestone is more beneficial. However, a milestone at a comparable step in the software development process says nothing about how close you are to finishing a project within the unpredictable world of software.

Preproject and postproject documents are often added because there is little of that kind of support in RUP, and various organizations handle these things differently. Your organization probably needs documents and procedures to handle the beginnings of projects, to set the commercial and/or legal aspects of assignments, to report to steering committees, or to handle the close of projects, among other things.

In Appendix B, "Adding Another Project Management Method to RUP," we give you two samples of mergers between project management methods and RUP's Project Management discipline.

9.3   Changing RUP

Change RUP? Can you do that? Is it allowed? It depends on what you mean by *change*. Selecting parts to include, exclude, and add are natural changes when you configure RUP and build your process. But then it depends on what parts you are talking about. As long as the parts are *whole* roles, activities, or artifacts, you are very safe. It's when you "go inside" these and make changes to, for example, steps in activities and headings in artifact templates that things get trickier.

You should not change the *meaning* of various things in RUP. You should not change the meanings of RUP roles (e.g., don't let the software architect become a nontechnical role handling only business data architecture). You should not change the meanings of activities (e.g., don't change the step-by-step description in such a way that the original purpose of the activity isn't fulfilled anymore). You should not use artifacts to do things they weren't intended to do (e.g., don't use the Vision artifact template to document the project's time plan).

If you change things in RUP too much or, rather, change them the wrong way, it will get very confusing. People will have trouble understanding your usage of RUP. You will lose the benefit of RUP as a standard process that provides a common language. New hires and external consultants will have difficulties with "your RUP," and misconceptions should be expected. Also expect extra work when new RUP versions are released.

The basic rule about making changes to RUP is that if you have good justifications and the ability to explain your deviations from the original process, if everyone agrees that the changes will be made for solid business reasons, and if you do not deviate from the spirit of RUP—then it's acceptable to make changes to RUP.

9.3.1 Changing Activities

What changes can you make regarding activities? The meaning of an activity should not be changed; its purpose must remain intact. In this subsection we describe some "allowed" activity changes we have seen at various organizations. (Remember that the arguments for making the changes were very good and that it was easy to "trace back" to original RUP!)

Steps can be moved from one activity to another. One organization made changes in the Analysis & Design discipline to move the more trivial tasks of the software architect and the step for creating use case realizations, among a few more, to become activities of the designer role instead. The purposes of the involved activities stayed the same because the step didn't impact the purposes at all.

One activity can be split into two. In one situation, this arrangement was made, also in the Analysis & Design discipline, where the activities are written very generally so they apply to many kinds of technical environments. Most organizations have stated a standard platform that more or less every software development project should use. Refining the Analysis & Design activities and describing them given this mandatory standard platform is time well invested. The use case design activity was split into two activities: use case design of GUI and use case design of business logic. This split reflected the fact that design work at this organization always was split into two different teams with different competencies. Of course, these two teams needed to cooperate, and there were special steps for this in the refined activity descriptions. Also, they shared the same design model.

9.3.2   Changing Templates

Changing RUP templates is very common. Usually at least an organizational logo is added. But then the approaches differ. Some organizations state, "We will not change the templates at all. It's too expensive to maintain our own versions of them." Other organizations spend time adding and removing headings as well as translating the templates into their local languages. If you translate the templates, beware that if the version of the RUP product you're using is in English, the gap between the artifacts and the corresponding RUP activity descriptions may get too wide.

Making changes to templates is acceptable. Some people even recommend that you do so. Our recommendation, however, is that you don't. We have seen so many strange variants of, for example, use case specifications, where people invent subflow chapters, remove the alternative flows chapters completely, include headings for technical exceptions from the database, and so on. So stay with the originals. You don't have to write text under all the headings. Keep the headings you are not using at the moment; mark them as "not used." Also mark headings you've added. By doing this, you can easily handle new versions of RUP, and people who already know RUP will better recognize its elements.

9.3.3   Changing the Lifecycle

Changing the lifecycle is mostly a matter of adding things. Changing the meaning and evaluation criteria of the existing RUP milestones is basically not acceptable (except for incremental delivery; see below). However, adding an extra milestone is fine, as is not performing the whole lifecycle. Adding an extra phase? Probably not acceptable; we explain why below.

Let's look at three examples of a changed lifecycle. The first example is the incremental delivery lifecycle (see RUP, Concepts: Iteration) in which a single construction iteration is followed by several transition iterations that add more and more functionality. The meaning of the RUP milestone between the Construction and Transition phases has changed because a ready-to-use system will not be provided as the original RUP milestone states. Only parts of the final system will be delivered, parts that, of course, are expected to be valid and to work to some extent. But this is a change of the milestone evaluation criteria anyway.

A second example appears in the scope of RUP's mapping to one of the project management methods described in Appendix B. The prestudy project was conducted for only the Inception and Elaboration phases of RUP. Of course, a prestudy project can be nearly anything, but if it might be followed by the development of a software product, it is a good idea to use RUP and its recommended work order from the start. But beware that if you do only paperwork in your prestudy project and no coding, you are *not* following the RUP lifecycle, hardly even the Inception phase. (Using RUP puts you under a few obligations, such as early coding!)

A third example of a changed lifecycle is one where contractual work forces a buy decision as early in the lifecycle as possible. Alternatively, a relationship between an acquirer (orderer) and a supplier may force an early order placement. In these situations, many people find that none of the existing RUP milestones match their needs. At the end of Inception, too little is known about the software solution, its costs, and so on, whereas finishing the whole Elaboration phase is not a feasible alternative because this results in excessive costs for the supplier if no contract is given (or if no order is placed). Adding an extra milestone in the middle of Elaboration is probably the best alternative (see Figure 9.2).

Finally, is it acceptable to add an extra phase? For example, now and then we have met people who suggest an extra phase beyond Transition, named Maintenance. But this alters the RUP scope, which is restricted to a single software development project (or assignment, if you like) developing a certain product release. Maintenance also results in the development of

| Inception | Elaboration | Construction | Transission |

Time

Figure 9.2   *Adding an extra "buy decision" milestone in the Elaboration phase for a contractual project (or an "order placement" milestone in an acquirer–supplier situation)*

product releases (versions 1.1, 1.2, 2.0, and so on), and the normal RUP process can be used in that situation. Better than adding an extra phase is to simply run through the ordinary RUP lifecycle again and to do what you need in order to pass the milestones. Depending on the size of that effort, this second pass is sometimes called a Maintenance cycle or an Evolutionary cycle (see Kruchten [2001]). Most likely it will be much easier to fulfill the RUP milestones this second time as you are familiar with the problem domain the software should provide solutions for, as you already have a working architecture, and so on.

Of course, the actual staffing, time, and resources needed will not be the same as when developing version 1.0, but RUP activities *still* need to be performed and RUP artifacts *still* need to be produced (or updated). Instead of adding an extra phase, we recommend that you write a sample development case, or maybe a conceptual roadmap (see Chapter 10, "Documenting Your Process"), that focuses on maintenance and helps people understand how RUP is used under the circumstances of maintenance. (For example, RUP practitioners performing maintenance need to understand that when RUP says "find," "create," or "produce," they are probably better off reading these words as "find," "add," or "update," respectively.)

9.4   How Can a Mentor Help You Decide upon Your Process?

Building your own organizational process is not easy. It does not happen overnight. The process must be worked out, tried out, and built up in real software development projects. Process experiences from these projects will be collected to create the organization-level process. This will be discussed in more detail in Chapter 10, "Documenting Your Process."

A RUP mentor can speed up the time needed to build a suitable process by adding his or her experiences from former RUP adaptations. Common mistakes can be avoided, and the mentor can present some alternatives that have proven to work before.

The results from an organizational assessment (see Chapter 4, "Assessing Your Organization"), which can clarify an organization's situation, are a very good start for a RUP implementation. Using this information, along with dialogues with key persons involved in the RUP implementation, the mentor can suggest areas of the software development lifecycle that should be addressed first, and, some months later, what should be addressed as a second step. Building and implementing the process then take place more or less in parallel. (Note that this is recommended even if there is no RUP mentor.) The mentor helps with RUP knowledge and facilitates the change from old ways of working to new ones. This will be discussed in more detail in Chapter 11, "A Guide to Successful Mentoring."

9.5   Conclusion

When selecting parts of RUP to include in your own process, you can select different starting points. You can choose to base the selection on disciplines or best practices, or maybe artifacts or activities. Whatever you chose, there will be some benefits and some drawbacks. Make sure to think through your situation before starting the work. You might have process material that you want to use in addition to what can be found in RUP; if that is the case, RUP can be extended easily. When it comes to changing the information in RUP, some types of changes, such as alterations to templates, are easier to do then others, such as changing the definition of a project's lifecycle. When adding or changing material, consider that the process must be easy to maintain in the future.

In the next chapter, we will discuss different ways to communicate the decisions you made, that is, how to document your process.

10

Documenting Your Process

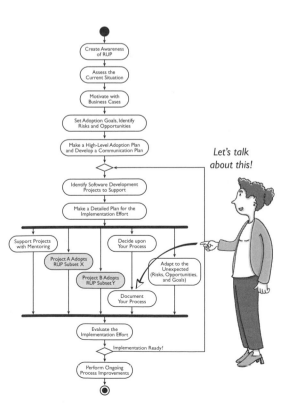

Let's talk about this!

In the previous chapter we discussed some options for adapting RUP to your particular situation. Based on the skills and demands encountered in your organization, information about RUP, and experience from software development projects, decisions have been made about what process should be used. Do people in the organization know about these decisions? Hopefully most people know something about the main changes that will occur, but the organization still needs to make all the information available by providing appropriate documentation of how the selected process currently looks. People might have different interpretations of the information gathered from meetings, workshops, and so on; the organization needs a common base to fall back to. Also, to make the process "future-proof," new employees will need the documentation to get up to speed.

The options you have for documenting a process span from traditional documents to sophisticated Web sites that look just like RUP itself. You need to familiarize yourself with the alternatives and to consider which alternative to choose in different situations. Because most organizations care about costs, the following factors typically impact the choice of documentation:

- The effort needed to write and create the documentation (relates to creation)
- The ease and possibilities of maintaining[1] the documentation (relates to creation)
- The skills and time needed to understand the documentation (relates to use)
- The number of people who need to read the documentation (relates to use)

Basically, you should not spend a lot of time documenting the process if it is not worth it. Process documentation is not a process. But because it is important that the RUP practitioners perceive the process documentation as supportive, some effort needs to be spent in making it appealing and most of all useful. The RUP practitioners of the process will often see only the documentation of your adaptation; at least, that will be the first thing they see regarding the process. Therefore, it is important to make your documentation clear and easy to understand. That doesn't always mean that you have to spend lots of time on documentation. Placing additional information in a guideline document stored "beside" standard RUP may sometimes be preferable to seamlessly merging additional information into the "proper" RUP activities. In fact, in our experience, *RUP practitioners often want to know what parts of an organization's process are standard RUP and what has been added and altered by the process implementation team!*

This chapter explores the documentation tools available when creating process documentation. Note that Chapter 9, "Deciding upon Your

---

1. Regardless of the format, it is important to make the description *maintainable*. As time passes, the needs of the organization will change, the RUP process used in the organization will develop, and the implementation environment might be replaced. It is imperative that you choose a description of the process that can be updated with minimal effort. If not, the process documentation will slowly become a description of yesterday's way of working. Project members will find the documentation less useful and eventually will stop using it at all.

Process," covers the subject of choosing what your process should be. Now we change perspective and explore what the RUP practitioners will face, i.e., the documentation results.[2] Finally, we put it all together and present a typical scenario showing how process documentation is built in stages.

10.1 Documentation Tools

In order to document and present a process—presumably one based on RUP (although none of the tools require that)—you may use one or more of the tools discussed in the following subsections.

10.1.1 Word Processor

In its most basic form, a document includes only a simple bulleted list or similarly brief notes—no headings, no introductory text, no pictures. Sometimes this can be appropriate process documentation. A document can also be more "proper" and use a certain document template (e.g., from RUP), have a revision number, include a history of changes, and feature well-prepared, extensive explanations and pictures. Documents may be stored on a common server or in a configuration management system, and users may reach them via links from Web pages.

You can use a word processor to create such traditional documents for RUP artifacts (e.g., the development case, project-specific or organization-wide guidelines and templates, and many others not particularly related to process documentation).

10.1.2 HTML Editor

Traditional documents may be stored in HTML format to make them easier to access over an intranet. You may also use an HTML editor with graphics and layout functionality to develop a sophisticated Web page, and perhaps you'd like to put together a "handmade" Web site with links to various kinds of information.

---

2. Some of the documentation results are RUP artifacts and some are not.

Using an HTML editor lets you create a project Web site or organizational shell (also a Web site, but *not* a process Web site generated with RUP Builder) as well as everything you may document with a word processor.

Should you put your process documentation on the Web or in a traditional document? The quickest and least expensive choice is probably to stay with a traditional document. This is suitable in small organizations, and it is a good start for larger organizations. The Web, however, has many advantages. For example, a Web site makes it easier to navigate between an organizational-level and a project-level process. Guidelines, checklists, templates, and so on can be reused more consistently. Also, a project Web site can create a combined source for the process used and the actual project documentation.

10.1.3   RUP Builder

The RUP Builder tool lets you generate a process Web site with the same navigation functionality as the standard RUP Web site: tabs with tree browsers to the left (known as *process views*), search engines, standard fonts and frames, and so on. Probably you will include quite a lot from the RUP base[3] as part of your process Web site, and if you decided to use content packaged in one or more RUP plug-ins, you will load these.

RUP Builder lets you create the development process artifact and edit the content of its related aid, the process views. Read more about this in "What the RUP Practitioner Will See" later in this chapter.

RUP Builder applies to projects that have or will use a project-specific development process to document the presumed process. If so, a development case refining the development process is not always necessary. Remember that the information on which artifacts, activities, and so on will be used also appears in the project's iteration plans. However, projects that use the organization-wide development process "as is" need a development case.

When presenting to the practitioners the subset of RUP you have chosen, you may decide to "cut out" the parts *not* included in that subset completely. The parts excluded will then be invisible in the process Web site.

---

3. You may have decided to use the Small, Medium, or Large (Classic) preconfigured RUP subsets for your process (see Chapter 9, "Deciding upon Your Process"). If so, you may fine-tune your choice by selecting/deselecting disciplines, process components, and even atomic process elements as activities, artifacts, and so on.

Alternatively, you may use the process views to highlight the selected subset and place the "not to be used" content on a "rest tab" or similar. Now people can still find and read the excluded parts if desired. *If you cut out things completely, you can count on the fact that some people will wonder what you have hidden from them!* We know of an organization that had its own test method and consequently used it to replace all of RUP's Test discipline. But people felt insecure, curious, or whatever—so the ordinary RUP Test discipline was made available for people to browse. (People won't automatically work according to the process description they see anyway!)

RUP Builder can always be applied at the organization level to generate the organization's customized RUP Web site after using RUP Organizer (see below).

10.1.4 MyRUP

By using the MyRUP functionality included in every process Web site generated with RUP Builder (including standard RUP), every RUP practitioner may document his or her own *process view* into the common process Web site. Frequently used descriptions in RUP can be made easier to access, and extra links to useful Web pages and documents on the Internet and intranet can be added.

A process creator may find it useful (if allowed) to "peek into" people's personalized views in order to harvest things to include in the organizational process and spread them to other people or projects.

10.1.5 RUP Organizer

RUP Organizer lets you connect description/text files with the underlying process model of RUP (or to your own process elements; see "RUP Modeler," which follows). You work in RUP Organizer if, for example, you want to add your own use case model guidelines and present them in conjunction with RUP's full description of the use case model artifact. Or you could add a good example of a use case written by someone in your organization right at RUP's description of what a use case is. You can package such "lightweight" additions to RUP into *thin plug-ins,* which just attach things to RUP's standard process model. RUP Organizer is the tool to do this! You also need a word processor or an HTML editor; when you are done, you proceed in RUP Builder, where you load the plug-in and generate your new Web site.

Adding your own examples, guidelines, and so on "inside" RUP, right beside the actual artifact or activity description, may be a good way to lure people into the RUP Web site, where plenty of good stuff waits for them. Unfortunately, people normally spend very little time reading RUP, so it doesn't hurt to give them extra opportunities to do some exploration on their own.

RUP Organizer can always be applied at the organization level to package the organization's own process information. A rather process-mature organization needs to do this at the start of the RUP adoption in order to include descriptions of existing processes and methods or at least things like programming guidelines, architectural policies, and so on that are used currently and very likely will be useful even when RUP is implemented. Still, the utmost advantage of RUP Organizer during a RUP adoption and implementation comes when using it to include the "fresh" experiences from projects that have adopted (parts of) RUP in combination with the exiting way of working at the organization.

10.1.6   RUP Modeler

RUP Modeler lets you create your own roles, activities, and artifacts and group them into process components. You may even model your own lifecycle, phases, disciplines, workflow details, tools, and tool mentors in RUP Modeler. You can package such "heavy" additions into *structural plug-ins*.[4] When done with the modeling, you proceed in RUP Organizer to add textual descriptions that finalize the plug-in. Then you may load it in RUP Builder to generate a Web site.

RUP Modeler may be applied at the organization level, but it is unlikely to be the first thing you use during a RUP adoption. You will probably have plenty to do to implement the RUP basics first. Also, using a simpler tool (a word processor) is a better idea in the beginning because your early additions will likely be sketchy ideas that will change a lot.

But eventually, after you've reached a point when your extra process content has settled and has succeeded in a real project, you'll want every other project within your organization to use it. With RUP Modeler and RUP Organizer, you can give your extra process content a notation and appearance that every RUP practitioner feels comfortable with. Using RUP

---

4. You may also hear people call it a *modeled plug-in* or a *thick plug-in*.

Builder and the organization's intranet or the Internet lets the resulting plug-in make its way to every single project team in your organization quickly and easily.

Both RUP Modeler and RUP Organizer are normally overkill to use within a project if it's not very large and long, but typically a project implementation team (see Chapter 7, "Obtaining Support from the Organization") uses them to package things harvested from projects.

As you've now seen, you can choose from many different tools and techniques to document your process. It may seem confusing, but in the same way that software engineering benefits from being automated by tools, process engineering benefits as well. During a process implementation, good pedagogical descriptions help, but remember—a process description is not a process.

10.2   What the RUP Practitioner Will See (Documentation Results)

Let's change perspective, leaving the tools behind and looking at the process documentation as it appears from the RUP practitioner's perspective. What's important for a practitioner? In our experience, practitioners want to see what parts of the process come from standard RUP and what has been added by the organization. Also, practitioners need help understanding "the main thread" of the process (which is tricky one for a RUP mentor to handle because there is no single main thread explanation that will work for every individual!). It is also very important to provide examples of every artifact[5] you are asking people to produce. In this section we sort out the various appearances of the process documention.

10.2.1   Development Process, Development Case, and Iteration Plans

These three RUP artifacts, in various ways and levels of details, tell members of a software development team what to do.

---

5. Except for the artifacts from the Implementation discipline, no programmers have ever asked us for sample code. (They understood they wouldn't get any, of course.)

The *development process* is the organizational process Web site that typically includes the RUP base (or a subset), additional process content from one or more external plug-ins, and material harvested from projects that have adopted parts of RUP so far. The purpose of the development process is to document the decisions about how to use RUP and other process elements and to make these decisions available to people in the organization. The development process typically covers the whole organization, but odd projects within your organization may need a development process of their own. RUP practitioners browse the development process for support and guidance. RUP Builder can be used to generate the development process.

The *development case* is a refinement of the development process and lists the roles, activities, artifacts, and tools to be used in a particular project (see Figure 10.1). A development case may be reused by projects that have very similar characteristics and circumstances. Every project should have a development case, but if the roles, activities, and so on will appear also in a project's *iterations plans* (see Figure 8.4), the RUP practitioners get a second chance to find the same information (and will survive without reading the development case!). A development case is typically stored in a traditional document; some organizations store it as a Web page to make it easier to find and navigate.

If a development case will be used on the organizational level as a way to express an organizational process, you should give extra thought to its content and structure because the number of readers will increase compared with a development case used only on the project level. In Chapter 9, "Deciding upon Your Process," we discussed different choices of things (artifacts, activities, solution components, and so on) on which you can base the RUP selection. Even if, for example, you chose artifacts as a basis for selecting parts of the process, that doesn't necessarily mean that artifacts should be a basis for *presenting* the process to the users. In some extreme cases, the template for the development case in RUP has been simplified to such an extent that only tables of artifacts and their review levels remain. This approach may be "correct," but it may lead to undesired behaviors, such as people focusing on the production of artifacts rather than on how they do the work needed to produce results. It is better to encourage people to focus on activities because the descriptions and guidelines in RUP supporting day-to-day work are structured along those lines. Performing activities in the way they are described in RUP enhances each individual's capability because it encourages the

1. Introduction

1.1 Purpose

To describe the RUP-based process in terms of what roles, activities, and artifacts apply to this project. Look in RUP for detailed guidance on each of them. They will appear again in one or more of this project's Iteration Plans.

1.2 Scope

Project LS. N.B. No details given on working method in areas (disciplines) where RUP isn't adopted.

1.3 References

Ref 1   RUP

Ref 2   Project Assessment Report: Project LS

2. Overview of the Development Case

2.1 Lifecycle Model

2.2 Disciplines

Only disciplines where Project LS has the biggest needs for process support are covered:
- Requirements
- Configuration Management
- Test
- Project Management
- Environment (always involved when adopting RUP!)

3. Business Modeling

RUP's Business Modeling will not be applied in Project LS.

4. Requirements

RUP's Requirements will be applied as follows:

RUP Roles	RUP Activities	RUP Artifacts	Tools
System Analyst Requirements Specifier Requirements Reviewer	Develop Vision Find Actors and Use Cases Detail a Use Case Structure the Use Case Model Detail the software Requirements Capture a Common Vocabulary Review Requirements	Vision Replaced by Doc. X Use Case Model, containing Actors and Use Cases (described in one Use Case Model Survey and one Use Case Specification per Use Case) Supplementary Specifications Glossary Review Record (not in RUP's Requirements, but needed)	Word proc. A. Modeling tool B

The requirement artifact are produced and should be reviewed as described below:

Artifact	Incep.	Elab.	Cons.	Trans.	Reviewed	Tool
Actor	x	x				
Boundary Class						
Glossary	x	x				
Requirements Attributes						
Requirements Management Plan						
Supplementary Specification	x	x	(x)			
Use Case	x	x	x			
Use Case Model	x	x				
Use Case Package						
Use Case Storyboard						
User Interface Prototype	x	x				
Vision						
Actor (Report)						
Use Case Specification (Report)	x	x	x			
Use Case Model Survey (Report)	x	x				
Use Case Storyboard (Report)						

Figure 10.1   *An extract of a project's development case*

person to seek information about the work to be performed. Also, show-ing only the artifacts in the development case might undermine the statement that RUP is not a document-centric process.

In any case, you should always remember your audience: the RUP practi-tioners! Whether you prepare a customized process Web site to be your development process or use development case documents, people in your organization need to find information when they need it, and you need to present it in a context people can use as they perform their tasks. Some-times a process Web site is the best choice, sometimes traditional docu-ments are just as good—ask the people who will use the information!

10.2.2   Guidelines and Checklists—Easy and Valuable

Some organizations may have a situation that makes creation of an orga-nization-wide, common development process too big of an effort. There are even organizations that will not benefit from such a process, at least not at first (e.g., an organization that has several departments that cur-rently perform work in completely different ways). In this type of organi-zation, a good approach is to first align the ways of working by introducing common guidelines and checklists before starting the more formal intro-duction of a new process. Smaller organizations may never get to the stage of needing a customized development process, but they can still be aligned to the basic thoughts of RUP. You can use guidelines and check-lists to set the baseline of how to perform software development.

A *guideline* describes how to work with a concept of software develop-ment. Examples of guidelines included in RUP are listed below.

- Use case model guidelines describe how to avoid functional decom-position and how to use concrete and abstract use cases.
- Generalization guidelines discuss inheritance in design.
- Test ideas for method calls guidelines help the reader learn how to avoid that part of the code that remains untested.

A *checklist* can be related to a specific artifact, to a milestone, or to just about any other concept. The goal with a checklist is to make sure that everyone in the organization creating the same type of results reaches the desired quality level and that no information or steps are forgotten. The checklist does not tell the project members how to perform the work, just how it should look when it is done.

Guidelines and checklists are a good way to describe a low-level process in a small organization or a first step in a larger organization, and they can also be references to an organization-wide development case. For example, the development case tells you that the use case model should be created in the Inception phase and updated in the Elaboration and Construction phases. A checklist can define what state the model should be in at the different milestones. In the larger context, guidelines and checklists serve as hands-on descriptions of how to perform work during specific tasks.

10.2.3   Templates and Examples—People Love Them

Maybe people don't like ordinary document templates that much, but they do like—if not love!—*examples*. People want to start from something. It doesn't matter whether the example isn't perfect or whether it suits the new situation only fairly well. Making all artifacts from former RUP projects available for newcomers to browse is a good idea. But when documenting an organizational process, you should also put some effort into writing about specific examples that are particularly good in terms of being "RUP-ish."

You can provide RUP practitioners with *templates* containing not just headings but also prewritten body text. One organization we know did this with its software architecture document (SAD) template to help people with this rather difficult-to-write document. The organization had a tough architecture policy that every application developed had to follow, so many SADs shared some of the same content. Placing this shared content into the template helped people save time when writing SADs.

10.2.4   Roadmaps and Process Views—Help People Find Their Way

RUP is very extensive. To people who have just started to get acquainted with RUP, it might seem overwhelming and even impossible to find information in it. But the development case is there to help you, right? A development case explains how RUP will be used in a certain project or a certain organization. If you start reading the development case, it should be easier to grasp RUP, especially the parts of RUP that will affect you—or is it? The problem is that a standard development case is structured around disciplines; thus a good understanding of RUP is a condition for reading a development case. Beginners need a more "simplified" presentation of how RUP will affect their work.

Here is where the concepts of a *conceptual roadmap* and—quite different—*process views* come in handy as ways to help practitioners understand

RUP. The goal of conceptual roadmaps is to help people grasp the "main thread" of RUP. Process views may be used to help testers, requirements specifiers, and so on find all the parts of the process that affect them and their work.

A *conceptual roadmap* is structured along the phases of a project. Everyone employed in the software industry knows what a project is, so that is a good starting point. A roadmap is designed to describe how RUP can be used to address a certain problem domain. Examples of roadmaps that exist in RUP today are "working on small projects" or "developing e-business solutions." It is also possible to imitate those and create roadmaps that address "software development at organization X" and "software development for project Y." These roadmaps can be the starting points for all RUP beginners working in that organization or on that project. The details are then found in the organization's development process or the project's development case.

A *process view* appears as a tab with a tree browser to the left in the RUP Web site or any other customized process Web site generated with RUP Builder. A process Web site typically has a set of different process views set up, each of them pointing out a chosen subset of RUP. In standard RUP, there are process views prepared for managers, analysts, developers, testers, and so on. You may stick with this role-based division and add other material useful for your organization. Or you may prepare other process views, perhaps covering what's useful for a particular department, for a project adopting part 1 of RUP's Requirements discipline, for a project adopting part 2 of RUP's Requirements discipline and part 1 of the Test discipline, and so on. The options for helping your organization's RUP practitioners find their way are many.

People may also help themselves. In the personal process view (the MyRUP functionality), people may create their own favorite view into the process and other things they find useful.

10.3   Building Your Process Documentation in Stages

Your organizational development process should grow or, better, be fine-tuned and contain more and more appropriate support and guidance as you proceed with the RUP adoption. As long as your project teams improve the way they develop software, you will have good experiences to collect and to document. In the collaboration between the project level and the organization level, your process documentation is built in stages.

When the change in the organization is complete, you should have a well-supported organizational development process and a track record of successful development cases from completed projects. The most efficient way to define the organizational process, however, is to start on the project level. This might seem surprising, but one of the most common traps when introducing RUP is to spend too much time documenting a process for the organization before making sure that it actually works in the projects. Below we discuss a few stages that the documentation can go through as well as how development cases can move from one stage to another.

10.3.1 Stage 0: The Development Process Before the Adoption Starts

This stage is only for very process-mature organizations that want to gather what they already have in terms of guidelines, processes, and so on within the software engineering area, before the actual RUP adoption starts in one or more real projects. Because we have seen some organizations get stuck here (one of them for two years!), we want to issue a warning for this stage: Avoid spending too much time on this stage; do start/select a project to adopt RUP as soon as possible. People will have plenty to learn, and you might as well start implementing the RUP basics before you put into place your ultimate business process including RUP for software development.

What about tools? RUP Organizer and RUP Builder might be useful at this stage. You could also use an HTML editor to create an organizational shell (a traditional Web site) including the standard RUP Web site and other useful information about the RUP adoption to come.

10.3.2 Stage 1: The Development Case for the First Project

Before defining the process on the organizational level in any detail, start a project to try some of the overall process decisions you have made. In the development case for that project, it should be made clear in what situations RUP should be used and when other process material should be consulted. The project team itself might want to create project-specific guidelines and templates in addition to this. Note that a good practice is to

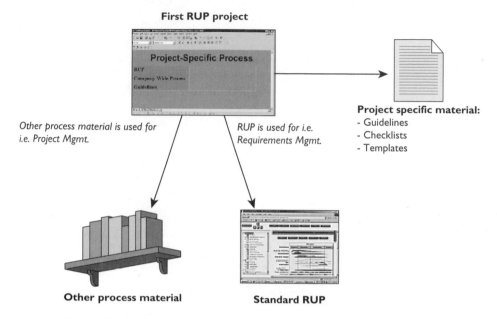

Figure 10.2   *Stage 1: the development case for the first project*

write the development case as you go and not complete everything at the beginning of the project.

The project team members use word processors for documenting the development case. If they benefit from the content of a certain RUP plug-in, they will generate a project-specific development process to include that.

After completion of the project, the actual project result is evaluated. In addition, the development case, other process documentation, and people's experiences and attitudes about the process need to be evaluated. As explained in the next section, the first draft of the organizational development process will be based on the experiences gathered from the first project. Figure 10.2 summarizes the stage 1 documentation.

10.3.3   Stage 2: The First Draft of the Organizational Development Process

The process decisions that worked well for the first project are reused on the organizational level. This makes them available for everyone in the organization. Some decisions might not have been optimal, and in that case feedback from the project team should be used to reconsider or fine-tune those. The templates and guidelines developed by the project team can also be added to the organizational level together with some sample artifacts.

RUP Organizer is used to attach the project team's guidelines, templates, and so on to the appropriate process elements of the RUP process model. RUP Builder generates the Web site. The HTML editor is used to update the organizational shell.

The purpose of an organization-wide process should be to define the basic rules for how projects should be performed in the organization. In order for the process to become the organization's *own* process, it has to be proven in the organization itself; no theoretical work can replace real experience. If too much time is spent on documenting an unproven process, the risk of meeting negative attitudes from the project team members will increase. It is also easy to fall into the trap of "documenting what I do not know," meaning that a process engineer documents steps in a process he or she has never performed. Figure 10.3 shows the status of the documentation after the first project has been run.

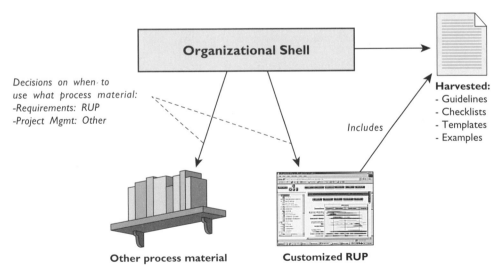

Figure 10.3   *Stage 2: The first draft of the development process on the organizational level, based on experience from the first project*

10.3.4   Stage 3: The Next Project Using the Organizational Development Process

The next project and others that follow can now reuse the experiences gained by starting from the documentation on the organizational level. Probably not all of the decisions about the process have been tried yet, and projects likely need to do more than the documentation on the organizational level says. After running the new project, those experiences will be added to the organization-level documentation. Running through a few iterations like this over time creates good documentation for the organization, and that documentation will be proven through actual project work.

A development case for a project should comply with the organizational development process (and vice versa). Every project is unique in some respect and needs a slightly different process. The development case for a project should refer to the organizational development process; it can add information to it and even deviate from it. The rules for how this can be done need to be stated on the organizational level. Elements added on the project level should be added to the organization level when proven successful. After every project ends, the organizational development process is updated when needed to reflect project experiences. At first, the changes will consist mostly of extensions of the first draft; later they will focus more on rewriting and replacing parts of the development process as the organization gains new experiences.

Depending on the kinds of experiences encountered during the RUP adaptation, RUP Modeler might be used to document additional roles, activities, or artifacts that a project has found is needed. RUP Organizer and RUP Builder then follow.

Figure 10.4 shows the relationship between the development case of the new project and the organization-level documentation from stage 2.

10.4   How Can a Mentor Help You Document Your Process?

The first time you document an adaptation of RUP, you are likely to fall into one or more traps. Among the most common are the following.

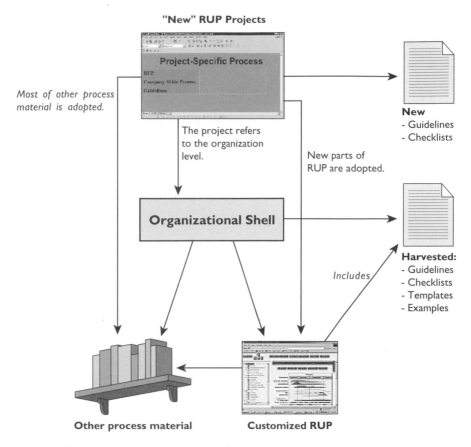

Figure 10.4 *Stage 3: The relationship between a new project's development case and the organization-level documentation*

- *Detailing too much before trying out the adaptation in a project.* The process needs to be proven in the organization to become widely accepted.
- *Documenting things you have not mastered.* Do not think that a process engineer will be able to describe the best way to work with all disciplines of software development.
- *Making too much of RUP mandatory.* Project teams will have different situations, and a too-rigid process will be perceived as a burden and not as a support to the project members.
- *Succumbing to "artifact hysteria."* Artifacts should help you on the way toward your goal, developing a high-quality software system. Artifacts on their own have little value; hence, artifacts that do not add value in

the project-specific situation should not be created. If the goal is forgotten and people start focusing on the next artifact to produce, the project may go into a mode where everything revolves around artifacts in a hysterical way and unnecessary artifacts are being produced.

A RUP mentor, who has seen or even fallen into these traps before, can help you avoid making these common mistakes. A mentor can guide you toward finding the appropriate documentation tool as well as writing an end documentation that suits the needs for the RUP practitioners without being too cumbersome to create or maintain. You could benefit from having the mentor actually write parts of the process documentation, but it is extremely important to keep the ownership of the process and its documentation inside your organization. In many of the most successful adaptations of RUP, the use of an external mentor has accelerated the adaptation in the beginning. Among other activities, external mentors typically help write the first drafts of, for example, a development case or a guideline. As soon as possible, your own employees take ownership of the process documentation and continue evolving it as a task among all the other tasks necessary to spread the process in the organization. Read more about the knowledge transfer between external and internal mentors in the "Performing Mentoring" section in Chapter 7.

10.5   Conclusion

The organizational process documentation starts off by reusing the development case of the first project to adopt RUP. Experiences, templates, examples, and so on are made available for future projects. After the conclusions of each project, more process material is harvested. This can be done by building more and more content into a process Web site or by using one or more of the tools for process authoring that ship with RUP.

In the next chapter, we will go into depth on why mentoring is important when changing an organization's ways of working.

11

A Guide to Successful Mentoring

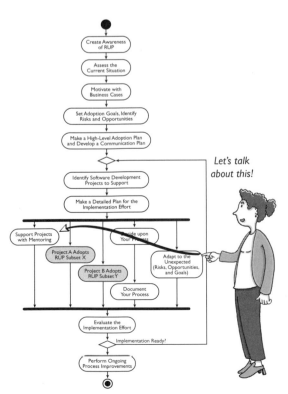

Let's talk about this!

Mentorship is essential to the success of the knowledge and skills transfer process that lies behind every successful RUP implementation. Instruction books can convey only so much knowledge. They cannot substitute for working side by side with someone who has already gone through the process. To some extent, you will need a RUP mentor when adopting RUP.

What is a RUP mentor? What can a RUP mentor do? What should you expect from a RUP mentor? We assert that a successful implementation of RUP is based on successful mentoring. It is often said that mentoring accelerates the implementation of a process and tools, but we want to sharpen that message a little and say that mentoring makes a successful implementation possible. Without mentoring, the

183

chance of success in terms of improved results regarding quality and productivity is small.

What is expected to happen when implementing RUP? The employees of an organization are supposed to abandon their existing viewpoint on how software is developed and switch to a new one: the RUP viewpoint. They need to change their current way of working—do things differently, do them in another order, or sometimes even do completely new things that they have never done before. And meanwhile, these employees should continue to deliver systems at least as good as before if not better. (At least, their managers will expect quick improvements.) During process implementation, the life of a software developer becomes very demanding![1]

But this is where RUP mentors can help—by making life easier and ensuring that the organization, its projects, and its employees come through the implementation and see the improved results they expect RUP to give them. The employees need knowledge and they need help making changes. The goals of RUP mentors are therefore twofold.

1. Transfer knowledge.
2. Facilitate change.

11.1   Knowledge Transfer

While transferring knowledge, mentors share their experiences about how to use RUP and the supporting tools in order to improve the results achieved in a project or in an organization. The concept of *knowledge transfer* can be a little bit misleading, and we want to clarify it once and for all because it triggers some questions.

Can knowledge be transferred? How is knowledge actually created? Knowledge has to be created within each person individually, and every person is unique. Unfortunately, an actual transfer or transmission of knowledge as portrayed in science fiction, where someone's brain gets connected to a computer or to another person's brain (see Figure 11.1), does not work.

---

1. But in the end, life will become less demanding because RUP gives you structure, guidance, and so on.

Figure 11.1 *Unfortunately, transferring knowledge is not this easy.*

Transferring knowledge is not that easy nor as rapid as it sounds; it needs to be adjusted to the situation and to the individuals involved.

Is it possible for a RUP implementation to succeed without mentoring? No—if you don't want to be just a simple follower of rules,[2] you need a mentor. The term transfer may make you think there is not much knowledge to talk about. If a simple transfer can be done, the amount of knowledge cannot be very extensive, and therefore it shouldn't take long to figure it out on your own, right? But the mentor will help you see behind the rules and to head for a goal instead.

Does RUP already contain everything you need to succeed? Well, when it comes to factual knowledge, RUP is pretty exhaustive. RUP describes many concepts and terms, plus a good framework of instructions, or rules, about how software should be developed. But as mentioned earlier, some

---

2. You can think of RUP as a set of rules about how to behave when developing software. (A law book contains a set of rules about how to behave in a society.)

knowledge you cannot easily read yourself. A critical area of knowledge is the *practical application* of RUP—how to follow the rules in a certain situation and how to determine which parts of RUP best apply to that situation within an organization or a project. This kind of judgment is very hard to make without former experiences of applying RUP. Naturally, rules about how to follow rules are not found in RUP because RUP cannot possibly be aware of every situation that will occur. Nor is it possible to express everything in words. For example, even if RUP says that every project should have a software architecture document, there may be situations when a project should omit that document. Normally, you can't safely do this kind of rule breaking as a RUP beginner because you do not have the necessary experience. A RUP mentor with experience from many other situations and many other projects has seen the consequences of many choices regarding how to apply RUP. The mentor remembers these and knows which rules are safe to break as long as the goals for the project are achieved. Therefore, the mentor can help a project team make appropriate choices and, even more important, transfer his or her knowledge about how to understand and reason in a particular situation.

Mastering RUP is at least as complex a process as developing software. Complex problems require complex solutions. Let a mentor help you find the right parts of RUP to use and the right way to interpret those parts. Let the mentor take you beyond the stage of an advanced beginner (see the next subsection) to higher levels. Let the mentor share his or her experiences so that you can use your own judgment next time.

To convince you of the importance of a mentor and especially the phenomenon of transferring knowledge, let's explore the concept of knowledge a little and refer to some established theories.

11.1.1   How Is Knowledge Created?

How do human beings learn? As children we learn things like walking, talking, and eating nicely by imitating our parents and by trial and error. After a lot of practice, we finally master these skills. As adults we can choose other methods. We can read on our own, or we can attend a course where a teacher presents theories and instructs us in some arranged exercises. We can try to perform something in real life and learn from our mistakes, until we finally come up with the perfect paper airplane (see Figure 11.2). But many of the things we want to learn as

Figure 11.2 *Practice makes perfect.*

adults—like salsa dancing or running a use case workshop according to RUP—we do by instruction.

In epistemology (i.e., the branch of philosophy concerned with the nature of human knowledge), a book written by Hubert L. Dreyfus [1972], *What Computers Can't Do*, is very famous. In that book,[3] Dreyfus presents five

3. Also in his article "A Phenomenology of Skill Acquisition as the Basis for a Merleau-Pontian Non-representationalist Cognitive Science" from 2002, available at http:// socrates.berkeley.edu/~hdreyfus/pdf/MerleauPontySkillCogSci.pdf.

levels that normally are passed when learning a new skill.[4] The *five levels of skills* according to Dreyfus are *novice, advanced beginner, competent, proficient*, and *expert*.

Before explaining these skill levels, let's take a quick glimpse at what skills are required when developing software (for more on this, see the next subsection, "What Knowledge Is Needed?"). Developing software requires a number of *skills*, many of which are described in RUP (e.g., creating a use case model requires special modeling and analysis skills). Also, RUP suggests that a lot of work be performed in workshops (e.g., a use case workshop), which requires skills in how to act as a workshop facilitator. Apart from skills, *knowledge of facts* (e.g., the definition of a use case) is required. Factual knowledge is often needed to master a skill. Another kind of knowledge, known as *knowledge by acquaintance*, involves having sound judgment and can also be a condition for some skills (e.g., developing a development case).

The *novice* recognizes only simple *features* (or *facts*) and is given *rules* for determining actions on the basis of the features, Dreyfus states. He gives the example of a student car driver who learns to recognize such features as "speed indicated by the speedometer" and is given rules such as "shift to second gear when speedometer needle points to 10." A comparable RUP example is a novice use case modeler who recognizes "human beings" and is given the rule that "actor is a symbol that shall be used for users of a system."

Dreyfus states that blindly following rules produces poor performance. He also points out that a car would probably stop if the driver shifts too soon on a hill or if the car is heavily loaded. A RUP example of bad performance is a novice use case modeler who models every job title as a separate actor, even though the individuals with those titles use the system in exactly the same way.

The *advanced beginner* not only knows facts but also has a better understanding of the *context* in which the facts make sense, Dreyfus continues. After seeing a sufficient number of examples, the learner begins to note— by himself or with the help of an instructor—meaningful additional *aspects* related to the facts. Dreyfus equates this to the student car driver

---

4. Dreyfus also argues that computers (i.e., expert systems and artificial intelligence systems) can never reach levels as high as humans do, but that is another story!

who starts to listen to the engine sounds when shifting gears. A RUP example is a use case modeler who understands that in relation to the system being modeled, different job titles can play the same role. Hence they should be modeled with the same actor.

But still at this level, Dreyfus explains, people only follow rules, though the examples they are given continuously increase their experience. Characteristic of advanced beginners and novices is that *they feel little responsibility for what they do—they only apply rules, and if they fail, they blame the rules instead of themselves.* During RUP implementations, we have recognized this behavior many times: people who blame RUP for one reason or another.

The *competent* person, Dreyfus states, chooses a certain *perspective* or works out a *plan* in order to cope with the overwhelming number of potentially relevant aspects he or she has learned to recognize. This perspective or plan—found by experience or by instruction—helps people distinguish between which aspects are important and which are not and to make understanding and decision making easier. At this level, Dreyfus says, car drivers no longer just follow rules; they drive with a goal in mind. If there is an emergency situation, a competent car driver could focus on getting to the intended destination, ignoring such things as passenger comfort and the law.

Dreyfus tells us that the rules and reasoning procedures necessary for deciding which plan or perspective to adopt are not easy to come by. In any domain, there are many situations, and a complete list covering every possible situation cannot be prepared. Therefore, competent performers must decide themselves, depending on the situation, what plan or perspective to adopt. They will not be sure that their choice will work out properly—which is a bit frightening. Because the result depends on their choice, they will indeed feel responsible. *This level is also the most emotional one;* there is an emotional investment in the choice of action, and people will naturally be frightened, excited, disappointed, or discouraged every day depending on their results.

The *proficient* performer, Dreyfus says, is absorbed within the world of his or her skillful activities and *sees* what needs to be done but must *decide* how to do it. Memories of similar experiences in the past trigger plans like those that have worked before. (When it comes to RUP implementations, this is—hopefully—the level we would place ourselves!)

The *expert* not only *sees* what needs to be achieved, Dreyfus continues, but also intuitively *sees* what to do. Experts have a mature and practiced understanding and immediately do what normally works—and, of course, it normally works.

The five levels of skills give us an understanding of how much an individual knows about a certain thing. When a mentor carries out knowledge transfer, the receiver of this knowledge—the RUP learner or apprentice—will be at one of the levels. As the apprentice gets exposed to more and more examples, more and more situations, he or she becomes more knowledgeable and capable and raises his or her skills one level at a time. The mentor guides the learner through all this by giving instructions, sharing tips and tricks, helping the learner to concretize problems, and exposing him or her to various alternatives. Some people need more guidance than others to reach a higher level; it all depends on the former experiences and knowledge of the RUP learner. Depending on what part of RUP is in question, the same individual may be on various levels, which is natural because RUP is broad and embraces all of software development. There are no possibilities of shortcuts through the levels, but a mentor really can speed up the process and help people become skillful much faster. And based on our experience, some people—and we also dare to claim some organizations—will never reach level three, competent performer, without help from mentors.

11.1.2   What Knowledge Is Needed?

When adopting RUP, every practitioner (project member) needs to have some knowledge about RUP. What knowledge in terms of *scope* is needed? Basically, every person needs to know enough in order to perform his or her day-to-day work in an efficient and successful manner. Practitioners typically wonder: "What parts of RUP affect me?" "What artifacts am I supposed to use to document my work?" "Do I know all the necessary functions of the tool I am using?" "Who am I supposed to work closely with?" Every person involved in a RUP project is in charge of one or more RUP roles, and practitioners can find that kind of information in the project plan, the development case, and of course in the role descriptions within RUP.

But what *kind* of knowledge is needed? In the last section we introduced three categories that epistemologists often use:

1. Knowledge of facts (or propositional knowledge)
2. Possession of skills
3. Knowledge by acquaintance

We have explored the theories of various philosophers and epistemologists in an attempt to find evidence that our strong belief in mentorship is reasonable. It didn't take us long until we were convinced:

There are things that you cannot learn by reading!

Despite the information technology society of today, where you can find instructions and guidance for nearly anything, and despite RUP's thousands of pages of guidance on how to best develop software, *you will need a human being* to teach you some parts. Naturally, skills and knowledge by acquaintance need to be taught from person to person, face to face.

Propositional knowledge, "knowing that," stands for plain, factual matters. For example, "I know that a bicycle has two wheels," or, "I know that a use case is a sequence of actions that a system performs in order to give something valuable to an actor." You can find plenty of this kind of knowledge in RUP: definitions of terms and concepts, the fact that "a project needs to staff a number of roles," the fact that "you should have a software architecture document," and so on. (These facts can easily be learned by reading.)

You can also find many descriptions in RUP about *how* to do certain things, for instance, how to create a use case model or how to run a use case workshop. When work is successfully performed according to these descriptions, you master certain *skills*. (Compare this with knowing how to fix a puncture on a bicycle.) The descriptions express a kind of knowledge known as *possession of skills*, "knowing how." Note, however, that knowing the *description* of the skill is not enough; you must be able to *practice* the skill in order to say that you have that knowledge. (Things are sometimes easier said than done.)

Unfortunately, not all skills can be easily described. Think about riding a bicycle; this certainly is a skill that can be mastered, but how should you describe it in a reasonable way? Similarly, it is hard to describe the RUP activity (step) "unify your design classes" exhaustively.

The third kind of knowledge, *knowledge by acquaintance*, covers familiarity of the subject and the sound judgment that comes with that. This type of knowledge we normally gain by experience: "I know that it's fun to bicycle because I've enjoyed it myself." RUP examples of this include the ability to judge whether one or two use cases are preferred in order to describe a certain functionality of a system and the ability to judge whether or not the project members will master the process suggested in the project's development case. RUP cannot describe how you can apply RUP because RUP doesn't know about your particular project. It's up to you to come to a decision.

On the basis of our skills and our knowledge by acquaintance we can handle the variety of concepts and rules found in RUP. These kinds of knowledge are not visible, but without them the propositional knowledge never comes into play. If you're not able to apply RUP correctly, you won't be able to use the good ideas of RUP, and you won't experience the improved results in software development that result from a successful RUP implementation.

Can skills and knowledge by acquaintance be transferred from one person to another? Yes, but not (only) in a theoretical, written form. The primary form of this kind of knowledge transfer is in concrete situations where a knowledgeable person guides the less knowledgeable on the basis of concrete examples, *as in the relationship of a master and an apprentice.*

To summarize, all knowledge cannot be contained in RUP itself. RUP is a set of rules about how to develop software. The intention is that a RUP user should follow these rules. But RUP doesn't say anything about *how* these rules should be followed; it can be done in various ways and depends on the situation (the particular software development project). The guarantee that a rule will be followed in a proper way cannot be a rule itself. Following rules is a way of acting, a *practice*. However, it is possible to guide and mentor a beginner who tries to acquire control of a practice and the built-in concepts.

11.2   What Does a Good Mentor Do?

There are, of course, good and bad mentors. Methods and processes are an interesting area, and a lot of companies are on their way toward implementing RUP; seeing a business opportunity, many consultants seek their fortune by becoming RUP mentors. Some are better than others. Some have experience, some do not.

Apart from experience, whether or not a person is a good mentor also can be a question of personality. Because different organizations have different climates and manners, a mentor who is considered very good by the people at one company could actually be disliked by those at another. Changing ways of working is very emotional, so collisions due to "personal chemistry" happen now and then. But a practiced and skillful mentor can handle various personalities and situations.

But what distinguishes a good mentor from a bad one is not only a question of which skill level the mentor possesses or his or her personality—it is very much a question of what the mentor does. The actions you should expect from a RUP mentor are discussed in the subsections below.

But first, let us remind you that *adopting RUP is a change*. It is of utmost importance that the mentor be aware of the mental processes that people go through when exposed to changes. People's mental processes and the progress of the knowledge transfer go hand in hand during a RUP adoption. The RUP mentor, who will have daily contact with the software developers due to the knowledge transfer that needs to take place, is probably the most important "change agent." The RUP mentor needs to *facilitate change*, which likely will involve him or her in many discussions asking why RUP is being adopted. Read more about this in "Reactions to Change" in Chapter 5, "Motivating the RUP Adoption."

11.2.1   Walk Around and Be Present

It is very important that a mentor be present physically at the organization. The help must be close at hand. It is not good if an employee gets stuck for too long; irritation grows very quickly and hinders, or at least slows down, the implementation. There is always a solution, and the mentor can help people out in every situation.

Apart from always being available on the phone or in a room not far from the people adopting RUP, the mentor should walk around and engage in some small talk (see Figure 11.3). Why? People often have questions that, for various reasons, they do not ask if the mentor doesn't "happen to be there." Perhaps they fear they'll sound stupid. Perhaps they think their questions are too small and unimportant. Perhaps they are shy, or they don't like talking on the phone, or they don't like writing e-mails. Perhaps they are too lazy to leave their desk and walk those few yards to the mentor's desk and find that the mentor isn't there.

So a mentor should walk around and be present. Start conversations. Ask how people are doing. Tell them tips and tricks without being asked. Tell them what is usually difficult about their task. The mentor should use various forms of interactions: for example, talking, drawing on a piece of paper, standing up and drawing something on a whiteboard, and putting together a PowerPoint presentation to explain difficult issues.

As an example of the latter, many people in a project kept returning to the same question, "What is the main thread in RUP? It's so hard to see the main thread." The mentor produced a picture showing this graphically, which satisfied them. Now they knew that the mentor really listened to them, that their question wasn't irrelevant; it was possible to give an answer to it. They didn't waste any more time on the main thread issue; instead they spent their energy on other issues.

11.2.2   Encourage People

A mentor should continuously encourage and praise the people adopting RUP. People might not realize that they've produced some really good results if no one tells them. Encouraged people are likely to repeat their good work and are more willing to take new steps and learn new things. When people have confidence, life is so much easier; they feel safe, they feel good, and they're more likely to happily engage in the RUP implementation.

The mentor could take a look at what people have done so far and say such things as "That looks good," "That will do," "Those things are not so important," and "You got it now—perfect!"

11.2.3   Never Criticize

If someone has done something wrong, the mentor must be very careful about how to correct it. To embed the correction in praise is one trick, but first the mentor should ask herself or himself: Does it really matter that it's not perfect? Maybe certain things could be left out for now; there is a high possibility that the person will discover the errors later, perhaps in the

Figure 11.3   *A RUP mentor should be present and often walk around among the people adopting RUP.*

next iteration, without having them pointed out. But the mentor must beware that people are different. Some really want things to be as perfect and as "RUP-ish" as possible straight away. Then, of course, the mentor should tell them how to make it perfect! Others are struggling with many things and cannot take criticism of any kind.

However, there are a few areas where you cannot cheat at all, for example, you can't pass the Elaboration–Construction milestone without reaching the stated criteria. The mentor should save possible criticism to address problems related to the most important things in RUP ("Pick your battles!").

11.2.4 Practice What You Preach

Some people have the opinion that mentors should only talk, always keeping their hands behind their backs and never doing anything themselves. But this is not a good idea. Instead, mentors should show people that they know the practices they are talking about.

Mentoring by doing (writing) is sometimes much more efficient than just talking. As children we learn by imitation or by trial and error. Most of the time imitation comes first; children see how we do a certain thing and then try to do the same thing themselves. They may have to practice several times until they get it right. So do not complicate things—show an example! For instance, the mentor could ask for an electronic version of a use case specification, take some time to rewrite it according to all the advice he or she normally gives verbally, and hand it back. Then he or she could show the use case specification to the other requirements specifiers and ask them to describe their use cases in a similar style, which will result in good and homogenous use case descriptions very quickly.

The mentor should help the project group get going with the very important guideline documents by creating the documents and starting to write the first basic rules that everyone should follow when modeling analysis classes, for instance. Then the mentor should have another person take over the responsibility for the document and write down every decision made regarding how to behave in the analysis model. If a description of a certain RUP activity is very general and far from how the work will actually be performed, the mentor should show how to rewrite (specialize) that RUP activity in order to bring it closer to reality. Then the mentor can ask another person to do the same thing for another RUP activity. In this way the mentor can help many documents get started by writing first drafts of them. Sometimes it is very difficult to start something and much easier to continue it. But on the next project it shouldn't even be difficult to start the document because people will have written similar documents themselves in a previous project.

The mentor should be careful not to write too much. Remember that the employees must learn to do the writing themselves. The mentor should give examples and as soon as possible have others take over, supervising their work as long as necessary.

11.2.5　Be Prepared to Conduct a Workshop

Many activities in RUP are most effective when performed as workshops. Every workshop has a facilitator who has the responsibility of running the workshop. In addition to arranging the location, sending invitations to the correct people, and so on, the facilitator needs to know what to do during the actual meeting. How will the workshop begin? What will take place during the workshop? What questions will be asked, what things shall be written down and how? How can the discussion be guided in order to stay focused on the expected outcome of the workshop?

This way of working may be completely new to an organization. But it is a skill people need to acquire in order to work according to RUP. The mentor possesses the skill of running the workshops in RUP and should be prepared to do so. The mentor should also be prepared to transfer his or her knowledge about how to run a workshop to one or more of the employees. Let facilitator trainees take over as soon as possible.

11.2.6　Know Your RUP

A mentor must know all the concepts explained in RUP. Preferably he or she should know them by heart, but for some not so central concepts it could be acceptable to just know where to find the information in RUP.

The mentor should never just answer a question regarding concepts—he or she should also show where to find the information in RUP and how quickly and easily it can be found. Then the next time that person has a question, he or she will be able to retrieve an answer just as easily as the mentor did. Hence, knowing how to navigate in RUP is very important.

11.2.7　Know Your Limits

Nobody can know everything about RUP. Even the best mentor has limitations when it comes to details regarding certain activities and artifacts of a certain discipline. The mentor may know the facts stated in RUP regarding the topic but may lack real-life experience. In that case, a good mentor does not pretend to know the answers; instead, he or she arranges to consult with someone who has more experience in order to complement his or her own knowledge and skills. But if you happen to find a RUP mentor as described in Figure 11.4, you should be very grateful!

A dream RUP mentor:

- At least 10 years experience in software engineering
- Certification in RUP
- Expert knowledge of all parts of RUP
- Solid experience in implementing RUP in large organizations
- Experience in measuring methods such as CMM and SPICE
- Experience in Rational products

Figure 11.4   *Qualifications of the RUP mentor of your dreams*

11.2.8   Worry, but Be Happy

Remember the song "Don't Worry, Be Happy"? Almost the same goes for RUP mentors—the only difference is that they *should* worry. While supporting a RUP adoption, it is important to listen attentively and take action as soon as people have worries or show signs of resistance. This may be due to misunderstandings that can be clarified right away, but it could also be due to a poorly managed RUP implementation. The most alarming situation would be if the project team members feel that RUP hinders them from developing software. If this happens, the RUP mentor has done a bad job so far. Maybe the pace for the RUP adoption is too aggressive (too much change at once) or the suggested process needs to be customized in some way to suit the needs of the project team. If such a situation isn't handled, RUP will certainly get a bad reputation, and the adoption will be jeopardized. Never think that you have control—always worry and double-check.

On the other hand, a positive and easygoing climate during a change of process is vital. The RUP mentor should always be positive and happy about RUP and be sure to let everyone know all the good things about it. The mentor should clarify how helpful RUP is and infect people with enthusiasm. If something is fun, it is easier to adopt. However, the mentor has to be honest and tell people what parts of RUP many people find confusing and hard to understand.

11.2.9   Keep Up the Speed

It is important to have some speed in order to get somewhere. A mentor must make sure that a RUP implementation doesn't make projects slow down too much or, even worse, get stuck. So keep up the speed!

Remember that a general "rule" with RUP is to do as little as possible, but still enough. The mentor should help people distinguish between what is important and what is not. It isn't necessarily the most important thing to create the best analysis model in the world. It might not be worth spending too many hours writing the perfect test plan. Project members have time schedules to fulfill and they should often ask themselves: What is most important right now? For instance, sometimes the organizational development case must be sidestepped, no matter what its originators say.

11.2.10 Let People Make Mistakes

The mentor should encourage a working climate that is open minded and free of status consciousness, where it is acceptable to make mistakes. In a way, it is good if people make mistakes because such errors form a very good basis for learning.

Sometimes the mentor can let someone continue with something that began slightly incorrectly because he or she is quite certain that the person will soon realize the mistake half an hour later. If not, the mentor should carefully guide the person to correct the error and, if possible, arrange an opportunity for the person to do things correctly from the start on a similar case.

11.3   Typical RUP Adopter Personalities

Like all human beings, software developers are all different (surprise!). They have different ages. They have different levels and types of formal education. They have different interests, skills, and experiences. They react differently to organizational changes, method changes, technical news, and news in general. They have different attitudes toward their bosses, their workmates, and external consultants. They work for companies with different climates and cultures, which they adjust to and become part of in a way.

In order to give just the right support to every software developer during a RUP adoption, a RUP mentor has to be a good listener and must be at ease with all the different personalities that will be affected by the change. When heading toward the goal of adopting RUP, the mentor needs to get everyone on board as quickly and as smoothly as possible. The mentor will probably encounter some resistance. It might be necessary to prepare temporary "workarounds" when some people don't feel like doing what the mentor asks them to do according to RUP.

Although it could be dangerous to generalize, we have put together a short list of typical personalities that we usually come across when advising and mentoring. We reveal some tips and tricks on how to handle each personality type.

11.3.1   The Long-Time Employee

In organizations or companies that have been around for a while, you are likely to find people who have been with the company for a very long time. Some of these people might feel threatened by a RUP implementation in the beginning, but that is not always the case. They may also feel that RUP could make their company even better. It depends on how RUP has been presented to them. It is important to explain that RUP is "only" a process description; those who perform that process are more important. What is very crucial when building a certain kind of system is knowledge about the *domain* that the system will cover. Long-timers are a gold mine for domain knowledge, and their status becomes visible in the RUP roles they could take on.

A general trick when someone shows resistance to RUP is to involve that person in the discussion of what parts of RUP to adopt. Creating ownership will hopefully minimize resistance. If this doesn't work, the mentor can try to figure out an activity that the person will like (maybe creating a full domain model?). This activity might not be the most important one right now, but its outcome will certainly be useful when the implementation reaches a later stage.

11.3.2   The Architectural Guru

Organizations often have "gurus" of various kinds (e.g., architectural gurus). Sometimes gurus delay the creation and completion of their artifacts. It doesn't necessarily mean that their knowledge is not real; it could just be that they have a great resistance to writing. Perhaps the guru cannot express his or her knowledge in words.

Let the guru come up with the ideas and arrange for a junior employee to document the ideas in the software architecture document or whatever artifact is appropriate. (A fruitful side effect of this approach is the knowledge transfer that will take place between the two people.)

11.3.3   The Code Lover or Hacker

Hackers normally don't like processes because they think they'll have to write documents. (Hopefully they are not as disapproving of modeling, at least if the model can be reverse-engineered from the code with some help from a tool.)

Make sure to inform the hackers that their work is the most important work of all because they are making the code. No code, no system. Clarify that their job probably won't change very much. (The mentor can introduce the changes that *will* affect them case by case, just in time.) Clarify that there will be no "useless" documents for them to write if they are not involved with the choice of architecture. Interview them for things to capture in design and programming guidelines, instead of forcing them to write the guidelines themselves. (Sooner or later they will see the benefit of the guidelines and take over the responsibility themselves.)

11.3.4   The Test Person

Test persons are also a gold mine when implementing RUP. They are like police constables when it comes to keeping things in order. The iterative approach in RUP creates a need for an ability to manage change because there will be many internal releases, builds, and so on during the development cycle. The test persons put pressure on the developers to know exactly what is implemented, what bugs have been corrected since last time, what is still missing, and so on. Also, because the test persons use requirements (use case descriptions) as one of their main inputs, they will soon let you know whether something is strange, missing, or completely wrong. Of course, test persons must not hinder the delivery of creative solutions, but most often their early involvement increases the quality of the product being developed as well as the process used.

11.3.5   The Process Lover or Enthusiast

We agree that processes are fun, as are models and good documentation. But do not get too enthusiastic. Process enthusiasts may come up with very good development cases (where almost every artifact in RUP is marked as mandatory!) or figure out some very good additions to RUP, but then they will be surprised to discover that everyone else, those in the development projects who are supposed to do all these things, aren't as enthusiastic as they are.

Remember that the ones who are going to perform the work probably don't like it when someone tells them what to do and how to work in detail. A mentor or a process engineer has to choose a very careful attitude and work in close cooperation with the performers instead. This is also one reason for not spending too much time on adapting or configuring RUP in sheltered workshops. First, the configuration might not work in reality, and second, people who are expected to perform the work according to the configuration will feel no ownership at all.

11.4   A Mentor Should Become Redundant

How long will you need a RUP mentor? As long as there are new things left to learn, new employees to train, more parts of RUP to adopt, more skills to practice, and a desire to work even more efficiently and achieve even better results. Still, the goal for a mentor should be to become redundant, that is, to be needed no more. This aspect is important not only to ensure a successful knowledge transfer but also to limit expenses—an external mentor usually costs good money to hire.

Let's focus on how the goal of becoming redundant affects the knowledge transfer. Foremost, the mentor should strive to help his or her learners manage by themselves and become self-sufficient as soon as possible. A parent teaching his or her child how to drive a car does not want the youngster to master driving only when the parent is sitting in the passenger seat. In the same way, we do not want the RUP practitioners to never learn how to seek for information themselves in RUP. Therefore, it is important that the mentor not only demonstrate his or her knowledge by answering questions but also guide the RUP practitioner to the place in RUP that handles the subject in question. Once found, the topic should be discussed. The mentor could share tips, tricks, and former experiences; the learner could question the topic, try to understand it, and challenge the mentor with various presentations of problems.

Neither do we want a situation where the mentor acts as the workshop leader (facilitator) in every use case workshop a project team carries out.

This is an easy trap to fall into because the mentor is naturally the most skillful facilitator on a project full of RUP beginners. Of course, the mentor should run the first workshop in order to show how the process works, but before the workshop starts there should be an appointed facilitator trainee. The trainee then runs the next workshop while the mentor sits by and helps the trainee when necessary. After a while the mentor doesn't even sit in the room but is available outside or at least afterward for discussion and evaluation of the outcome of the workshop.

Children need some basic care and some rules to start with. But only when let free and allowed to try things themselves can children grow and reach higher levels. Their parents can be delighted and gradually end the responsibility of raising their children. The same relationship applies to RUP learners and their mentors. A RUP implementation is neither finished nor successful until the mentors are no longer needed and the RUP learners achieve results as good as if the mentors had been around. Sound mentors should at that point feel happy, satisfied, and relieved. Their mission has been completed.

11.5 Conclusion

Mentoring has two purposes: to transfer knowledge and to help facilitate the change that an organization goes through when adopting a new process. A mentor should help with the practical application of knowledge in RUP. You can't learn RUP completely just by reading; much of the knowledge is created when applying the theories in practice. When it comes to skills, a number of levels can be defined. People can move up this skill ladder on their own, but a mentor can speed the development of skills, and the highest levels might require mentor support to reach at all. To facilitate change, the mentor needs to be present. People need to be close to their support, which must be adjusted depending on each individual's personality. A mentor is great to have while learning new things, but the goal for the mentor must be that the people to whom he or she transfers knowledge should become self-sufficient.

Experiences from Actual Implementations

In this appendix we describe the experiences from two implementations of RUP, one by Volvo and one by Covansys.

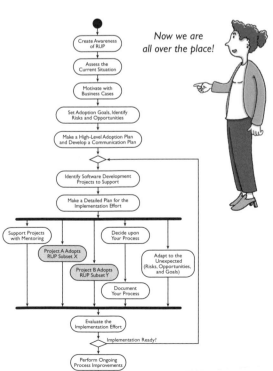

Now we are all over the place!

A.1 Volvo Information Technology

Volvo Information Technology [1](IT) is a subsidiary of the Volvo Group, which is one of the largest industrial groups in the Nordic Region, and provides all types of industrial IT solutions in a variety of technical environments. Volvo IT employs 4,300 persons

---

1. The text in this section is adapted with permission of Volvo from the Whitepaper "Implementing RUP in an Organization—The Volvo IT Approach," written by Göran V. Grahn and Boris Karlsson, 2002; see http://www.rational.com/media/whitepapers/rup_volvo.pdf.

globally. For a more complete description of Volvo IT's experiences, please refer to the whitepaper "Implementing RUP in an Organization—The Volvo IT Approach," on which the following text is based.

A.1.1   Background

Like many other companies, Volvo IT has experienced new challenges within the realm of application development. Some movements in the industry that affected the way Volvo IT looks upon software include the following.

* Software and business are becoming more and more integrated. Software used in an organization needs to produce a concrete value to the business. Hence, software development and business engineering need to be integrated.
* Businesses are changing more rapidly, and software development teams need to raise their productivity to keep up with the changes.
* Running a global business requires global solutions, so development projects must use participants who come from several regions of the world.

In light of these trends, the company concluded that Volvo IT needed a common process for application development that was integrated with existing processes for project management and business engineering.

Let's look into how Volvo IT is working with process improvements and how application development fits into that context. Three "layers" have been defined (see Figure A.1).

* *Method Strategy:* On this level, business challenges and objectives are analyzed, a Method Strategy is developed, and an expected outcome is defined.
* *Process/Method Development:* Based on the Method Strategy and specific implementation objectives, an evaluation and selection of the development process takes place, followed by the actual implementation. The results produced are analyzed and fed back to the Method Strategy level.
* *Application Development:* On this level, the actual development projects are run based on the selected process and application objectives. Besides the obvious result (the application itself), outcomes such as competence and experiences from RUP are measured and fed back to the levels above.

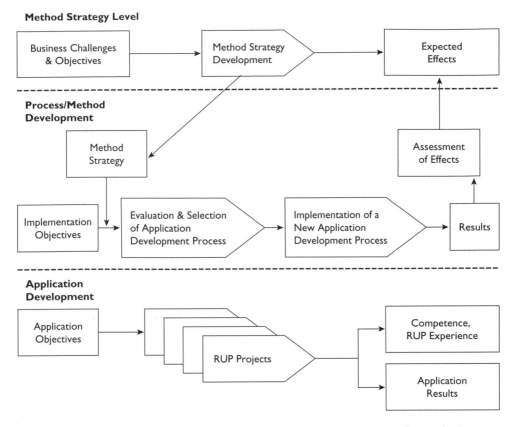

Figure A.1   *The software improvement process context (used with the permission from Volvo.)*

A.1.2   **Timing/Effort**

The target group for the implementation consists of a thousand people in total. The implementation project is staffed with a project manager and two people responsible for tools and training (working part-time on the project). A coordinator, who is appointed per unit or site, spends about 10–15% of his or her work hours with the implementation.

The *RUP coach* is expected to work approximately 150 hours per project and a total of 150 hours in preparation. Each *RUP specialist* is expected to work between 50 and 100 hours per project.

A.1.3   Long-Term Goals

By implementing a common process framework, Volvo IT expected to reach the following goals, among others:

- Determination of well-defined business requirements to use as input on development projects
- A better fit between product and business needs at time of delivery
- Less time needed to develop the first version of an application
- More projects completed on time and within budget
- Reduced cost of rework
- Better product maintainability
- One common process for all application development

A.1.4   Configuration

To begin with, the focus was to make people aware of the process and to implement the Requirements and Analysis & Design disciplines. After some time, the focus shifted toward implementation of two best practices (develop iteratively and manage requirements). The company learned that *it is neither possible nor recommended to implement all of RUP at once.*

A.1.5   Strategy

Volvo IT decided to *form a project to handle the implementation of RUP.* This decision was based mainly on the fact that it takes time to achieve a cultural shift in an organization of this size. In order for the organization to build experiences of using the new process in a controlled way, the implementation project used a "staged approach" where the first step (after initial preparation and piloting) affected about 10 projects and 60 developers. Step 2 roughly doubled these numbers, and step 3 (ongoing at the time this book was written) consists of about 50 projects and 350 developers.

One of the more important issues in the beginning of the implementation was to decide which projects should be the first in the organization to use RUP. The *RUP pilot projects* cannot be allowed to fail, so Volvo IT was very selective when choosing the projects. The following criteria were used.

- Size: Each pilot project should consist of a team of 3 to 10 people, last 3 to 9 months, and take 2,000 to 5,000 person-hours to complete.
- Criticalness: The pilot projects can't have a critical deadline. The time schedule must be allowed to have some slack in it to allow for the participants to learn the new process, methods, and tools. (Volvo IT estimated that at least 4 weeks of slack was needed.)
- Interest: The project manager and the team must be interested in and motivated about learning RUP.

The company defined a number of roles to support and control the implementation. Among the more important roles were the RUP coach, RUP specialist, and coordinator.

The *RUP coach* is responsible for supporting the use of RUP at his or her site. The coach gives practical assistance and also informs the employees about new development, plans, and results. A *coach network* was formed to give coaches the opportunity to exchange experiences with other coaches. In the beginning, external coaches assisted with the implementation and also trained the employees who would become internal coaches.

The *RUP specialist* is responsible for developing and improving support material (e.g., the configuration of RUP, templates, guidelines, and so on). The specialist also helps the coach support the project teams when needed.

The *coordinator* plans, manages, and monitors the use of RUP at his or her site. This role also helps the management find suitable projects to use RUP and coordinates with the coaches what support is needed.

Training programs were defined for different roles within the organization, both participants in the development projects and other staff, but it was soon realized that the project team members needed a more concrete knowledge tied to their actual projects than standard training could offer. With this in mind and to help the coaches in their work, a set of *configurable workshops* was defined with the purpose of refreshing the theoretical knowledge gained at the training courses as well as applying the knowledge to an actual problem.

A.1.6   Methods for Measuring Success

Volvo IT used several methods to follow up the investment of changing its development process. One method used *a questionnaire* to gain feedback from the project teams and customer representatives after each project was finished. The questions covered the people's experiences of RUP as well as training and coaching. The level of satisfaction was measured on a scale of 1 to 4, and the goal was to have 80% of the answers on level 3 or 4. This goal was exceeded by far. Among the comments from the questionnaires, the following stand out.

- "The focus on requirements and risks during the projects is especially appreciated."
- "The cost of maintenance is expected to be lower for products developed using RUP."
- "Implementing a new process is an investment in competence and must be regarded as a long-term improvement."

Another way to measure the success of the implementation was to show the success of projects using it. Volvo IT published several *success stories* in its internal magazine to share the experiences of the pilot project teams.

Even though questionnaires and success stories are a good way to get a feeling for the impact a new process has on an organization, it is not an objective method for measuring success. Volvo IT chose to *use the SPICE[2] method* to assess some project teams before and after the implementation of RUP. Together with the university of Borås in Sweden, the basis for such assessments was defined. This work resulted in Before/After Capability Profiles that were used to assess three projects representing different areas. The Before assessment was performed at the beginning of a project to assess how the project would be performed if RUP were not used. The After assessment was performed when the project was in the Construction phase of RUP. SPICE measures different areas on a scale from 1 to 5. The measurements at Volvo IT indicate that the implementation of RUP raised the capability from level 1 to level 2 for most areas. The following is a quote from the Volvo IT whitepaper: "The assessment result clearly indicates that the implementation of RUP is having an effect. However, there is a big

---

2. Software Process Improvement and Capability dEtermination (ISO/IEC TR 15504:1998). See the official Web page at http://www.sqi.gu.edu.au/spice.

potential for further improving the process capability with growing experience in RUP."[3]

A.1.7 Challenges, Traps, and What Could Have Been Done Better

Thorough planning before the implementation (which also included selecting what process to work with) revealed possible traps for the implementation. A list of "critical success factors" was defined as well.

- Management commitment: The commitment from top management needs to be "active."
- In-house process engineering skills: To keep the implementation aligned with the goals and on track over time, it is important to keep the control of the content and process variants in-house.
- Integration between processes, methods, and tools: The different methods and tools need to be consistent with each other and the process.
- Distribution: Realizing that the process needs to evolve over time, it is important to have an easy way to distribute new versions of it to the organization.

After completing the first steps in the implementation plan, Volvo IT shared these recommendations for an implementation.

- Make sure that management gives active and ongoing support.
- Use an implementation project to separate the implementation activities from the normal day-to-day work of the organization.
- Do not implement all parts of RUP in all parts of the organization at once.
- Establish well-defined roles and responsibilities for the implementation.
- Define packaged workshops to support the development projects.
- Treat the implementation of a new process as an investment in competence. Make an estimation of the profit.
- Do not underestimate the human factor—changing people's ways of thinking takes time. Be patient.

A.1.8 Biggest Achievements

By showing that the projects can get from capability level 1 to 2 by starting to use RUP, Volvo IT concluded that it will be possible to reach level 3 for

---

3. See http://www.rational.com/media/whitepapers/rup_volvo.pdf.

selected processes within two to three years. Experiences from other organizations raising the level of capability (most of the documented cases used the Capability Maturity Model, or CMM, method of measurement) show that improvements are noticed in reduced schedule time and effort as well as reduced numbers of defects. This together with the results from questionnaires and customer testimonials clearly indicate that Volvo IT is moving in the right direction.

A.1.9   Continuation

The implementation at Volvo IT is not yet finished. When it received the results of the evaluation of the first steps, management gave the go-ahead for the next step in the implementation plan.

A.2   Covansys Corporation

Covansys Corporation[4] is a global consulting and technology services company that specializes in industry-specific solutions, strategic outsourcing, and integration services. Covansys employed more than 4,500 people worldwide as of the second quarter 2003, and reported revenues for the 12 months of 2002 were $382.8 million. Covansys is an IBM Premier Business Partner.

A.2.1   Background

Covansys, founded in 1985 and headquartered in Michigan, pioneered the transparent blended model of offshore IT outsourcing. Covansys began outsourcing operations in India in 1991, becoming one of the first U.S.-based IT vendors in the world to integrate offshore capabilities into its value proposition. Its subsidiary, Covansys India, has more than 1,900 full-time employees at development centers in Chennai, Mumbai, and Bangalore that occupy 250,000 square feet. Covansys India has been assessed at Level 5 of the People Capability Maturity Model (PCMM). This is the second such distinction for Covansys; the company also achieved the presti-

---

4. The text in this section was edited from an internal Covansys document and is printed here with permission of Covansys.

gious SEI-CMM Level 5 rating on its first assessment in 1999 for two of its three offshore development centers. The company was also recertified on ISO 9001. Covansys is the recipient of the prestigious 2002 IBM Americas Business Partner Leadership Award.

Being such an active and successful proponent of mature delivery processes, Covansys focuses on addressing typical system integration challenges such as meeting customer needs, delivering with speed and quality, controlling costs, and gaining repeat business. Covansys executes project delivery using an onsite, offsite, and offshore development model either as a turnkey responsibility or as collaborative engagement with its customers' teams. In this model, it has to ensure that the teams in all locations understand the projects and their priorities—and that these teams communicate completely and clearly. Covansys has solved these tough challenges by adopting the RUP platform and IBM Rational Software tools. RUP's flexible software development process platform enables Covansys to deliver customized yet consistent software engineering guidance to each Covansys project team.

The following description presents Covansys's implementation of RUP within its consulting and delivery teams and at its client organizations. Project-specific development cases generally derive from the organizational implementations.

A.2.2   Timing/Effort

Covansys's Web-to-Enterprise Integration (WEI) and its traditional e-business services practice is responsible for educating the delivery teams in the implementation and use of RUP. Covansys has been integrating Web applications with core business systems since the Web began. In doing so, Covansys has been using RUP since its infancy as a formal iterative development model.

Covansys has a number of employees trained in RUP and IBM Rational Software tools, including Rose, RequisitePro, ClearCase, and ClearQuest. The training is an ongoing effort in order to meet the demands of a global IT services and consulting company. The organizational RUP implementation has also resulted in a Covansys RUP Web, which is a tactical RUP environment available on Covansys's extranet that can be used by all Covansys staff as an internal shared knowledge center.

A.2.3   Long-Term Goals

Covansys's long-term goals for implementing RUP within the company and proposing that implementation within its customers' software development projects include the following:

- Accurately estimate project effort and schedule for a given scope and quality
- Consistently deliver the scope and quality within the effort and schedule
- Professionally manage and fulfill customer expectations

A.2.4   Configuration

The configuration of organizationally implemented RUP within Covansys has been determined based on the practical needs of the project delivery teams. As an example, one scenario through the implementation of the Covansys RUP Web environment pertains to a Covansys project manager or responsible team member entrusted with running or mentoring all or part of a mid-sized (10–12 team members for 4–6 months) e-business (object-based) project. Figure A.2 from the Web environment depicts what this configuration addresses.

- **What is <u>RUP</u>?** (briefly explained—skip it if you know it!)
- **Project <u>Planning</u>** (will get you to prepare your project plans.)
- **Project <u>Phases</u>** (will get you to work through the four phases of the project. It has the necessary documents for you.)
- **Specific <u>Disciplines</u>** (e.g., Requirements gathering. This is for you if you only need to do some part of a project based on RUP.)
- **Project <u>Roles</u>** (for you to do your team selection.)
- **Projects <u>Artifacts</u>** (documents, etc. grouped under disciplines like Requirements, Analysis & Design, and others.)
- **Work <u>Guidelines</u>** (if you need guidelines for specific tasks in your project like how to run a Use Case Workshop.)

This web site has been designed to be as pragmatic as feasible. It is intended to be complete enough to get your job done in an efficient way. However, it is by no means a complete guide to RUP. We recommend that you refer to your version of RUP whenever you need further explanations.

Figure A.2   *Example from Covansys RUP Web—the purpose and configuration (Used with permission of Covansys.)*

A.2.5 Strategy

As a consulting company with SEI-CMM credentials, Covansys's strategy for RUP implementation is two-fold.

1. Continuously create, maintain, and enhance internal reusable RUP assets.
2. Implement RUP in client organizations and/or on client projects.

The next subsection explores the first part of this strategy.

A.2.6 Create, Maintain, and Enhance Internal Reusable RUP Assets

Covansys continuously creates, maintains, and enhances targeted internal assets that it leverages for RUP implementations across its domestic and offshore operations. These are primarily material assets (including a Multi-Site Management discipline) and human assets.

Material Assets These include a set of activities and artifacts that contains the core set delivered by standard RUP, augmented with a supportive set developed by Covansys for onsite/offshore projects. The core set of activities corresponds to all RUP disciplines with specific activities instantiated by project type. The core set of artifacts includes templates for a development case, business case, vision, use case, software development plan and its components, software requirements specification and its components, software architecture document and its components, and so on. The set of activities developed by Covansys to fulfill the needs of onsite/offshore projects corresponds to all RUP disciplines and also has an added discipline called *Multi-Site Management*, which is elaborated below. The set of artifacts developed by Covansys includes those necessary to support Project Management Institute (PMI) standards and the needs of Covansys's PMI-certified project managers. The artifacts also include those required by the Multi-Site Management discipline.

Multi-Site Management Offshore software development was considered an emerging paradigm during the past decade, but now it is being widely accepted. Covansys has done pioneering work in this area. That experience has been built into Covansys's configuration of RUP in terms of the Multi-Site Management discipline. The objective of this discipline is to facilitate the task of multi-site (onsite/offsite/offshore) management of RUP-based projects. The discipline supports an approach to managing a multi-site project that significantly improves the odds of delivering successful software using this paradigm, especially for offshore software development.

The purposes of multi-site management include the following:

- To provide a framework for managing software-intensive projects that are executed across multiple sites (e.g., onsite, offsite, offshore)
- To provide practical guidelines for planning, staffing, executing, and monitoring multi-site projects
- To provide a framework for managing the assembly-line development model, which imparts control and efficiency to multi-site projects

One example of activities within the Multi-Site Management discipline is the "Golden loop." This is a short-term, tactically controlled activity that ensures that the onsite and offshore teams step synchronistically through the assembly line of implementation, testing, and deployment of code. An example from the artifacts specific to the discipline is the Use Case Tracking State Machine, which the teams update to register the state of a use case during its lifecycle.

Material assets such as those mentioned above are published on Covansys RUP Web (available on Covansys's extranet) and can be used by all Covansys staff.

Human Assets Covansys's RUP implementation strategy relies heavily on its human assets—the professional women and men who are full-time employees at the various domestic and offshore locations. RUP-related roles are staffed by people with two types of skills: those suitable for RUP mentors and for RUP project staff members.

RUP mentors are responsible for implementation of RUP within Covansys and its client organizations at the organizational, enterprise, and project levels. Examples of this role are RUP implementer, CMM-RUP consultant, process mentor, process engineer, process review authority, and project management office staff.

RUP project staff members are responsible for executing onsite/offsite/offshore software development projects using RUP. Examples of this role are onsite/offshore project manager, offshore coordinator, system analyst, architect, designer, test designer, implementer, and tester.

Such staff members are typically chosen and trained based on their aptitude and performance in similar roles. The training is two-fold: educational and vocational. *Educational training* is offered through various channels, including classroom training and computer-based training. Select individuals are invited to take focused training and/or certifications on certain aspects such as RUP fundamentals, RUP implementations, specific disciplines of the RUP, and tools. *Vocational training* starts with on-the-job assignments working with Covansys's RUP experts. This mode of training continues until the person gains sufficient RUP implementation skills to work on his or her own. The person then contributes to a number of projects as RUP project staff. Only when the person is acknowledged as a leader in implementing RUP is he or she chosen to be a RUP mentor.

A.2.7 Methods for Measuring Success

Since Covansys implements RUP at two levels—by executing RUP-based onsite/offshore projects and by implementing RUP within organizations—the measurements of RUP implementation are in terms of the numbers of RUP-based software development projects and RUP implementation projects. These and the corresponding granular metrics are captured as a part of the project management office's processes that monitor various projects. Some of the measurements Covansys captures include the following:

- Number of onsite/offshore projects in execution
- Number of staff trained in RUP (overview)
- Number of staff trained in RUP disciplines (in depth)
- Number of staff trained in RUP-related tools
- Number of staff certified by PMI
- Other CMM/ISO-related project measurements

A.2.8 Challenges, Traps, and What Could Have Been Done Better

When Covansys implements RUP in a project, one of the major challenges is to focus on the software development project that should benefit from RUP without the RUP implementation becoming a project in itself. This is because the primary goal is to maximize the clients' return on investment on the software project.

When Covansys implements RUP in an organization or enterprise, one of the major challenges is to *manage the culture change* (e.g., from a waterfall paradigm to an iterative paradigm) that typically results from a RUP implementation. The other important challenge relates to *persistence of purpose*. Process adoption can exist for various purposes, including the real needs of the adopting organization on one extreme or individual vested interests on the other. Process adoption is a long-term investment by the organization and/or the individuals that can continue only as long as the purpose persists. Covansys builds in activities to ensure that the persistence of purpose is ascertained at various levels and at various times.

A common challenge Covansys faces in both project and organizational implementation of RUP is the need to answer the client's question: "What is in it for me?" This is also a breeding ground for traps. Some of Covansys's recommendations to a RUP implementation client are listed below.

- You are a "stakeholder" now!
  - Your planned, continuous participation is important.
- Learn to live with live documents.
  - Reviews and sign-offs of changing and growing documents should be accepted.
- Accept gradual solidification of requirements.
  - Around 80% of functional requirements will be known before the Construction phase.
- Accept gradual solidification of the design.
  - Iteration-specific design will be done during Construction.
- Resist the *how* when you discuss the *what*.
  - Don't engineer the design (*how*) while discussing the use cases (*what*).
- Construction is a set of sequential Iterations (i.e., mini-projects).
  - We will have frequent builds per iteration.
  - There will be one release per iteration.
- Accept objective progress reports.
  - These will be based on phases, iterations, and milestones.
  - These will not be based on a completed plan or design.
- Accept planning uncertainty.
  - RUP does not cause this, it only acknowledges it!
  - Normally no firm estimate of project effort or cost can be given before the Elaboration phase.
  - There will be two levels of the project plan:
    - One coarse-grained overall plan
    - Many fine-grained plans, each for the next Iteration

A.2.9   **Biggest Achievements**

Covansys's achievements related to RUP implementation at this time include those listed below.

- RUP and corresponding tools (including Rose, RequisitePro, ClearCase, ClearQuest, and others) have been successfully put to use within the company for execution of RUP-based onsite/offsite/offshore projects and projects to deliver RUP implementations in client organizations.
- A substantial number of staff members are trained on RUP, its disciplines, and corresponding tools.
- Covansys has taken the paradigm of offshore software development to the next level of formality by introducing a Multi-Site Management discipline in RUP that includes the activities and artifacts necessary for offshore software development.
- Covansys RUP Web on the company extranet offers practical configurations and guidance to Covansys's staff on RUP implementation.

A.2.10   **Continuation**

The e-business practice within Covansys is responsible for making sure that implementation of RUP and the corresponding tools continues to generate the software engineering excellence in which Covansys has its roots. Specific initiatives are planned to make this happen.

Adding Another Project Management Method to RUP

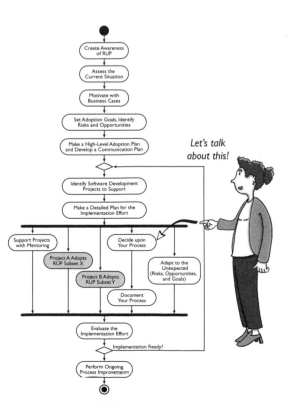

Let's talk about this!

In this appendix we briefly describe how two project management methods have been merged with RUP's Project Management discipline: PROPS from Ericsson, used in Ericsson companies worldwide, and PPS, developed by TietoEnator. You may read this appendix to get a hint about how to proceed when merging another project management method with RUP, a topic that first was introduced in the "Adding Process Information" section in Chapter 9, "Deciding upon Your Process."

B.1 PROPS

PROPS is described as a steering instrument used to strengthen an organization's business. PROPS gives support to the single project perspective, the project organizational perspective, the business perspective, and the human perspective. It is based on experiences from thousands of projects conducted at Ericsson during more than a decade.[1]

In a process-based organization, there are *operative processes* that refine input into a desired outcome and *management processes* that steer and control the operative processes. Normally projects are used for achieving major changes in the organization's operations, for instance, product development. The work performed within a project adds a *project management process* to the process map (see Figure B.1).

In PROPS, the single project flow is depicted as a U (see Figure B.2) in which a *project steering model* with six tollgates (TG0–TG5) is found in the outermost layer. A *tollgate* in PROPS is a predefined decision point at which the project sponsor decides how to continue the project based on project status, business situation, and use of resources. The six tollgates are outlined below.

> **TG0:** Initiation of prestudy.
>
> **TG1:** Shall the feasibility study be started?
>
> **TG2:** Shall the project be performed?

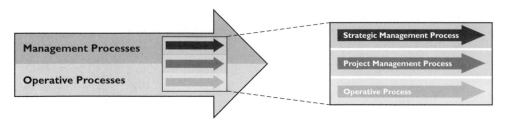

Figure B.1 *A project is part of the organization's operations. (Reprinted with permission of Ericsson.)*

---

1. PROPS is developed and owned by Ericsson AB and made available and supported by Semcon AB (http://www.semcon.se/spm). The text in this section is printed here with permission of Ericsson.

TG3: Shall the project continue with the original or revised time plan?

TG4: Shall the result be presented to the project sponsor?

TG5: Shall the project be approved and concluded?

The next layer contains a *project management model* divided into four phases holding activities for project planning, team building, control,

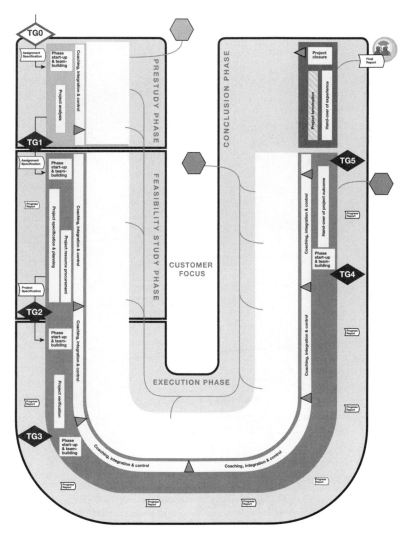

Figure B.2   *The PROPS U symbolizes the single project flow. (Reprinted with permission of Ericsson.)*

and so on. Finally, the innermost layer represents a *project work model*. But this layer is empty—therefore inserting RUP here works perfectly well.

In PROPS, the correlation between phases and tollgates is fixed, with the Prestudy Phase between TG0 and TG1, the Feasibility Study Phase between TG1 and TG2, the Execution Phase between TG2 and TG5, and the Conclusion Phase beyond TG5. However, in each project, the project sponsor and the project manager should agree upon suitable times for the tollgate decisions and what information the project sponsor needs for the decision. This means that the mapping to RUP cannot be fixed. Where a tollgate is placed in correlation to RUP's milestones depends on the type of project.

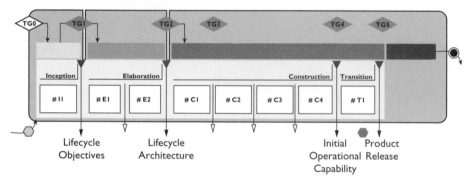

Figure B.3   *PROPS–RUP mapping for incremental development (Reprinted with permission of Ericsson.)*

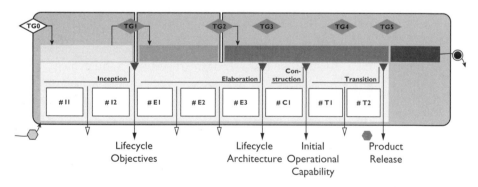

Figure B.4   *PROPS–RUP mapping for evolutionary development (Reprinted with permission of Ericsson.)*

Two sample projects show how the PROPS–RUP mapping can vary. The first one, *incremental development*, develops a product with mature and well-known technology and known customer expectations (see Figure B.3). The second one, *evolutionary development*, is a high-risk project with new technology and an unclear business case (see Figure B.4).

B.2   PPS

PPS is described as a well-proven working method for actively controlling and managing projects.[2] It is generic and independent of the type of result a project will produce. Combining PPS with a development model, or a *production model* as it is called in PPS terminology, is a natural thing to do, and combining PPS with RUP works well. Separated from a project's production model, you find the *management model*, which is the center of PPS.

The PPS management model defines eight different decision points (DP1–DP8) that describe a *project* lifecycle that every project will pass (or not).

DP1: To start the project and provide a framework up to DP2/DP3 (project directive)

DP2: To continue with more detailed preparations

DP3: To approve the project's preparations (requirement and solution descriptions and project definition)

DP4: To produce the agreed result

DP5: To continue with or change the project's commitment

DP6: To approve the project's result or partial result for use

DP7: To approve transfer of the result from the project to maintenance

DP8: To conclude the project.

The decision points need to be mapped with RUP's milestones and phases, which describe a *product* lifecycle. (Note the difference from above: project lifecycle versus product lifecycle.) For a development

---

2. PPS is from TietoEnator (http://www.tietoenator.com/pps). The text in this section is printed here with permission of TietoEnator.

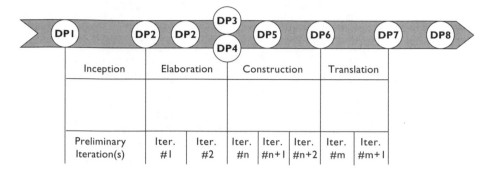

Figure B.5   *PPS–RUP mapping for a standard project (Reprinted with permission of TietoEnator.)*

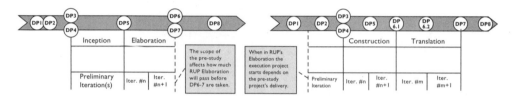

Figure B.6   *PPS–RUP mapping for a prestudy project (left) and an execution project (right) (Reprinted with permission of TietoEnator.)*

project running from idea to a finished product release, the mapping looks like that shown in Figure B.5. But because PPS is generic and not bound to what is produced, it works well to set up a two-project scenario where a prestudy project is (perhaps, not necessarily) followed by an execution project, as shown in Figure B.6.

Within PPS you will find many things that RUP lacks completely, like setting up a strong commitment and feedback culture, support for conflict handling, team-building activities, and other "soft" matters. Just use those parts of PPS as they are. But there are also areas where PPS and RUP overlap. An organization using both methods needs to make a number of decisions that finally come down to whether to use a PPS document template or a RUP document template. Table B.1 provides a few examples by listing RUP documents, their corresponding PPS documents, and recommendations for use of the RUP documents.

RUP Artifact (Document)	Corresponding PPS Document	Explanation	Recommended Use of RUP Document
Software development plan	Project definition	The project definition is basic to PPS.	Do not use
Iteration plan	Version/edition plan	The PPS version/edition plan is described in incremental and evolutionary development. However, PPS has no template, so use the RUP template for iterative development.	Must be used
Iteration assessment	—	There is no corresponding template in PPS.	Must be used
Status assessment	Project report	Use the PPS document.	Do not use
Business case	—	In PPS, the orderer is normally responsible for calculating return on investment.	Can be used
Configuration management (CM) plan	Project definition	Small projects describe relevant parts of the CM plan in the project definition. Larger projects may need to write their own separate CM plans.	Can be used

Table B.1   *Recommended Use of RUP Documents in a PPS Project. (Reprinted with permission of TietoEnator.) For a complete list refer to the whitepaper "An overview of PPS and RUP interaction" written by T. Vading and A. Ulenius, 2002; see PPS Online Demo on http:// www.tietoenator.com/pps.*

Glossary

In this glossary, "(RUP)" indicates that the definition comes from the RUP Glossary, with slight adaptations to fit the context of this book (with permission of IBM Rational Software). Items followed by "(UML)" are terms defined by the open standard Unified Modeling Language.

activity. a unit of work a role may be asked to perform. (RUP)

adoption. the activity of selecting parts of RUP and adding process material to create a process that fits the needs of your project and/or organization.

architect. the role in RUP responsible for the architecture of the software system.

architecture. the highest-level concept of a system in its environment, according to IEEE. The architecture of a software system (at a given point in time) is its organization or structure of significant components interacting through interfaces, those components being composed of successively smaller components and interfaces. (RUP)

artifact. a piece of information that: (1) is produced, modified, or used by a process; (2) defines an area of responsibility; and (3) is subject to version control. An artifact can be a model, a model element, or a document. A document can enclose other documents. (RUP)

assessment. the activity of evaluating the current capability of an organization or project to develop software. The result of an assessment is a report covering conclusions and recommendations. See Chapter 4 for an extensive description.

assessors.   the individuals performing an assessment.

business case.   a document (calculation) describing the economical motivation behind a certain action.

component.   a nontrivial, nearly independent, and replaceable part of a system that fulfills a clear function in the context of a well-defined architecture. A component conforms to and provides the realization of a set of interfaces. (RUP)

development case.   the software engineering process used by the performing organization. It is developed as a configuration, or customization, of the RUP product, and adapted to the project's needs. (RUP). Development case is often used for the actual document describing this process.

development process.   a configuration of the underlying RUP framework that meets the needs of the project following it. The development process can be organization wide or project specific. (RUP)

discipline.   a collection of related activities that are related to a major "area of concern." The disciplines in RUP include: Business Modeling, Requirements, Analysis & Design, Implementation, Test, Deployment, Configuration & Change Management, Project Management, Environment. (RUP)

domain.   an area of knowledge or activity characterized by a family of related values. (RUP)

framework.   a micro-architecture that provides an extensible template for applications within a specific domain. (UML)

guideline.   provides prescriptive guidance on how to perform a certain activity or a set of activities in the context of the project or organization. (RUP)

implementation.   (1) to put a process to use within an organization or a project; (2) also, a discipline in the software engineering process, the purpose of which is to implement software components that meet an appropriate standard of quality. (RUP)

increment.   the difference (delta) between two releases at the end of subsequent iterations. (RUP)

interface.   a collection of operations that are used to specify a service of a class or a component. (RUP)

iteration.   a distinct sequence of activities with a baselined plan and valuation criteria resulting in a release (internal or external). (RUP)

iterative process.   a process that uses iterations as the base for planning is considered to be iterative.

lifecycle. one complete pass through the four phases: Inception, Elaboration, Construction, and Transition. The span of time between the beginning of the Inception phase and the end of the Transition phase. Synonyms: development cycle, cycle. (RUP)

maintenance. the alterations or further development of a process or product after the initial development project has been concluded.

mentor. an individual who performs mentoring, a trusted advisor.

mentoring. the activity of transferring knowledge to practitioners while they are performing productive work.

milestone. the point at which an iteration formally ends. (RUP)

model. a semantically closed abstraction of a system. In the RUP, a complete description of a system from a particular perspective ("complete" meaning you don't need any additional information to understand the system from that perspective); a set of model elements. Two models cannot overlap. (RUP)

OMG. Object Management Group.

opportunity. antonym of risk. Something that can positively affect your ability to reach your goal.

pattern. a solution template for a recurring problem that has proven useful in a given context. (RUP)

PEP. Process Engineering Process; describes how to adopt RUP in an organization or a project.

phase. the time between two major project milestones, during which a well-defined set of objectives is met, artifacts are completed, and decisions are made to move or not move into the next phase. (RUP)

pilot project. the first project to use a configuration of RUP (or part thereof).

plug-in. a technique for defining process content specific to a certain domain, tool, or technology.

process. a set of partially ordered steps intended to reach a goal; in software engineering, the goal is to build a software product or to enhance an existing one; in process engineering, the goal is to develop or enhance a process model; corresponds to a business use case in business engineering. (RUP)

process engineer. a role that performs development, configuration, or adaptation of a process.

prototype. a release that is not necessarily subject to change management and configuration control. (RUP)

quality assurance (QA).   all those planned and systematic actions necessary to provide adequate confidence that a product or service will satisfy given requirements for quality. (RUP)

release.   a subset of the end product that is the object of evaluation at a major milestone. A release is a stable, executable version of product, together with any artifacts necessary to use this release, such as release notes or installation instructions. A release can be internal or external. An internal release is used only by the development organization, as part of a milestone, or for a demonstration to users or customers. An external release (or delivery) is delivered to end users. A release is not necessarily a complete product, but can just be one step along the way, with its usefulness measured only from an engineering perspective. Releases act as a forcing function that drives the development team to get closure at regular intervals, avoiding the "90% done, 90% remaining" syndrome. (RUP)

return on investment (ROI).   a calculation showing when money spent on something will be paid back.

review.   a group activity carried out to discover potential defects and to assess the quality of a set of artifacts. (RUP)

risk.   an ongoing or upcoming concern that has a significant probability of adversely affecting the success of major milestones. (RUP)

role.   a definition of the behavior and responsibilities of an individual, or a set of individuals working together as a team, within the context of a software engineering organization. (RUP)

RUP.   Rational Unified Process.

software development plan (SDP).   an artifact in RUP that defines the high-level plan for a software development project.

source line of code (SLOC).   a measurement traditionally used to describe the size of a software system.

subsystem.   a model element which has the semantics of a package, such that it can contain other model elements, and a class, such that it has behavior. The behavior of the subsystem is provided by classes or other subsystems it contains. A subsystem realizes one or more interfaces, which define the behavior it can perform. (RUP)

template.   a predefined structure for an artifact. (RUP)

Unified Modeling Language (UML).   a language for visualizing, specifying, constructing, and documenting the artifacts of a software-intensive system. (RUP)

use case.   a description of system behavior, in terms of sequences of actions. A use case should yield an observable result of value to an actor. A use case contains all flows of events related to producing the "observable result of value," including alternate and exception flows. More formally, a use case defines a set of use-case instances or scenarios. (RUP)

waterfall (model).   a model of the software development process in which the constituent activities, typically a concept phase, requirements phase, design phase, implementation phase, test phase, and installation and checkout phase, are performed in that order, possibly with overlap but with little or no iteration (IEEE). This definition applies in the RUP, with the substitution of the term "discipline" for "phase." In RUP, the disciplines are named Business Modeling, Requirements, Analysis & Design, Implementation, Test, and Deployment and in the waterfall model of development, these would occur only once, in sequence, with little or no overlap. (RUP)

Recommended Reading

Bittner, Kurt, and Ian Spence. 2002. *Use Case Modeling*. Boston, MA: Addison-Wesley.

Boehm, Barry W., et al. 2000. *Software Cost Estimation with COCOMO II*. Upper Saddle River, NJ: Prentice Hall.

Booch, Grady. 1996. *Object Solutions: Managing the Object-Oriented Project*. Reading, MA: Addison-Wesley.

Booch, Grady, James Rumbaugh, and Ivar Jacobson. 1999. *The Unified Modeling Language User Guide*. Reading, MA: Addison-Wesley.

Carnegie Mellon University, Software Engineering Institute. 1995. *The Capability Maturity Model: Guidelines for Improving the Software Process*. Reading, MA: Addison-Wesley.

Covey, Stephen R. 1990. *The Seven Habits of Highly Effective People*. New York: Simon & Schuster.

Dreyfus, Hubert L. 2002. "A Phenomenology of Skill Acquisition as the Basis for a Merleau-Pontian Non-representationalist Cognitive Science." Available in October 2003 at http://socrates.berkeley.edu/~hdreyfus/pdf/MerleauPontySkillCogSci.pdf.

———. 1972. *What Computers Can't Do*. New York: Harper & Row.

Fowler, Martin. 1999. *UML Distilled: Applying the Standard Object Modeling Language*, 2nd ed. Reading, MA: Addison-Wesley.

Göranzon, Bo. 2001. *Spelregler—om gränsöverskridande*. Stockholm: Sweden: Dialoger. (Available only in Swedish.)

Hammarén, Maria. 1999. Ledtråd i förvandling. Stockholm, Sweden: Dialoger. (Available only in Swedish.)

———. 1995. *Skriva—en metod för reflektion*. Stockholm, Sweden: Brevskolan. (Available only in Swedish.)

Janssen, Claes. 1996. *Förändringens fyra rum*. Sweden: Wahlström & Widstrand. (Available only in Swedish.) See also http://www.claesjanssen.com and http://www.andolin.com.

Johannessen, Kjell S. 1999. *Praxis och tyst kunnande*. Stockholm, Sweden: Dialoger. (Available only in Swedish.)

Kaplan, R. S., and D. P. Norton. 1996. *Translating Strategy into Action: The Balanced Scorecard*. Boston, MA: Harvard Business School Press.

Karlsson, Fredrik. 2002. *Meta-Method for Method Configuration* (Licentiate Thesis). Linköpings Universitet, Linköping, Sweden.

Klein, Peter D. 1998. "The Concept of Knowledge." In E. Craig (ed.), *Encyclopedia of Philosophy*, vol. 5, pp. 266–276. New York: Routledge.

Kroll, Per, and Philippe Krutchten. 2003. *The Rational Unified Process Made Easy: A Practitioner's Guide to the RUP.* Boston, MA: Addison-Wesley.

Kruchten, Philippe. 2001. "Software Maintenance Cycles with the RUP." Published on The Rational Edge, http://www.therationaledge.com/content/aug_01/t_softwareMaintenance_pk.html.

———. 2003. *The Rational Unified Process—An Introduction*, 3rd ed. Boston, MA: Addison-Wesley.

Reo, D. A., N. Quintano, and L. Buglione. 1999. "Balanced IT Scorecard Generic Model Version 2.0." Zamudio, Spain: European Software Institute.

Royce, Walker. 1998. *Software Project Management: A Unified Framework*. Reading, MA: Addison-Wesley.

Unhelkar, Bhuvan. 2002. *Process Quality Assurance for UML-Based Projects*. Boston, MA: Addison-Wesley.

Index